The Bishop's Wife

The Bishop's Wife

JASMINE CHRISTINE

authorHOUSE®

AuthorHouse™ LLC
1663 Liberty Drive
Bloomington, IN 47403
www.authorhouse.com
Phone: 1-800-839-8640

This is a work of fiction. All of the characters, names, incidents, organizations, and dialogue in this novel are either the products of the author's imagination or are used fictitiously.

Published by AuthorHouse   08/21/2014

ISBN: 978-1-4969-3513-7 (sc)
ISBN: 978-1-4969-3520-5 (hc)
ISBN: 978-1-4969-3514-4 (e)

Library of Congress Control Number: 2014914908

Any people depicted in stock imagery provided by Thinkstock are models, and such images are being used for illustrative purposes only.
Certain stock imagery © Thinkstock.

This book is printed on acid-free paper.

Because of the dynamic nature of the Internet, any web addresses or links contained in this book may have changed since publication and may no longer be valid. The views expressed in this work are solely those of the author and do not necessarily reflect the views of the publisher, and the publisher hereby disclaims any responsibility for them.

CHAPTER 1

"Holy, Holy, Holy. Lord God Almighty…" the King James Anglican Church choir rang out in melodious harmony the classic hymn penned by Reginald Heber. As the congregation rocked, they each belted out their personal version of the famous lyrics; some doing serious injustice to the music that John Dykes took great care in composing. Regardless, there was not a closed mouth in church that morning. It was Trinity Sunday, better known as "The Solemnity of the Most Holy Trinity" or the next Sunday after Pentecost. On this day, the church remembers and honours the Father, the Son and the Holy Spirit.

"Early in the morning, our song shall rise to Thee…" Tricia Dessington glanced around the packed church as she too sang with passion. As an Anglican, Tricia usually enjoyed a solemn service. Unlike the Pentecostals, Anglicans tended to be more reserved in their form of worship. Everything was almost always done with hymns and chants. Persons from other religions tended to view the Anglican way as a bit boring. For Tricia, church was anything but boring.

Her eyes moved over to the Lord's altar. It was beautifully adorned with fresh lilies and bouquets of colourful roses and a touch of baby breath flowers. Persons serving at the altar always moved with such grace and reverence. It was easy to fall into respectful trance as one partook in service. Tears welled in her eyes now as was customary these last few months. The pain in her chest engulfed her as she prayed to the Lord for deliverance from her sins. Tricia, the wife of The Most Revered Dr. Elias Dessington, was battling with some difficult yearnings for most of her life; after all she too was human. As she looked around the church, she reminded herself she was no different from the rest of the congregation.

1

They all had skeletons in their closet; some scarier than others. People always somehow expected the clergy and their family to be without sin; but this was hardly ever the case. The Catholic Church was recently catapulted to the limelight yet again as priests across various dioceses were found to be engaging in sexual activity with young boys in the church. The Vatican had one hell of a battle on their hands.

Tricia's gaze now landed on her beloved husband; the Bishop of Calvary Isle. They had been married now for twenty miserable years. No one would have guessed the pain Tricia felt daily; after all, her own husband was unaware. Not being one to start an argument, Tricia had suffered in silence… until recently. It's not that she didn't love her husband, on the contrary. She loved him dearly, but he just was never able to fully satisfy Tricia's sexual needs. As such, Tricia had sought to fulfil her wildest dreams and fantasies elsewhere. Now, someone, Lord knows who, had caught up with her, and was trying to shatter the very stability she had fought so hard to create and maintain in her marriage.

Shame overwhelming her, Tricia quickly glanced downwards as her husband's eyes met hers. Her mind journeyed to the letter she had received only a week ago. It outlined one of her more devilish encounters. Tricia had never prayed as hard as she did these last few days. Her position as the wife of the Bishop held her to high expectations. On this end, she always delivered. So when Tricia had decided she needed to step outside of the union to satisfy her ever rising sexual cravings, she had gone to great pains to ensure she was not caught. She respected her husband she believed, and the sanctity of the church; but she needed relief. Now, something had gone terribly wrong. Somehow her secret got out and she had no clue who the culprit was. When Tricia happened to open the strange looking letter on that fateful day, she nearly caught a heart attack. The letter, strewn with biblical verses reminding her of her oath to her husband before God, had outlined one of her recent escapades. Apparently, the mystery person had been in Cincinnati with her when she had gone to represent her husband at a function there. Knowing she was going to be away from home and that she knew no one in Cincinnati, Tricia had gone about her usual plans, now a habit, of arranging a meeting with one of the play boys from a nearby city. She was careful never to hire someone from the city she was in as she didn't want to risk them or herself being recognised. Her meetings needed to be discreet. Each one entailed a signing of a contract, large sums of money being passed for the benefit of secrecy, and the promise to give her the wildest sex she could manage. Forcing herself to withdraw from the memories of that session, Tricia sat for the delivery of the sermon with the rest of the congregation. Knowing exactly what her husband was about to preach having proofread the piece only the night before, Tricia allowed herself to recall just how she happened to arrive at her current sex addiction.

Tricia had always been a quiet girl. Growing up on a small island off the coast of Grenada, Calvary Isle, she was raised in the church by a very devout Christian mother and father. Every morning, they would sit around their simple kitchen and do their daily devotions as a family. This became a way of life for Tricia. At school she was usually the one expected to lead the class in prayers and song. The small Anglican school carried a student roll of mere 50 children. Seeing how small Calvary Island was, everyone knew everyone in that country. At secondary school she was active in all of the Christian groups and led several weekly services to raise awareness of the goodness of God to the young people on the island. It was no surprise then when main islander Elias asked for the opportunity to date the Godly beauty. Tricia made many trips to Grenada to see Elias. He had introduced her to the way of living of the main island. Calvary Isle, though small, operated as an attachment to Grenada. It had a thriving tourist industry as persons travelled from afar to enjoy the privacy of the beaches, the local foods and rich entertainment. When Tricia visited Grenada, it was a similar but enlarged version of Calvary. The native food was fantastic. Rich with the aroma of local herbs and spices. Well-seasoned meats adorned each plate, usually overflowing with tasty treats. But good food was not Tricia's weakness; it was the lure of the men.

"Let us prayer." The subtle request from her husband drew Tricia back in from her trance. They had travelled via ferry to Grenada only the day before. Elias had been invited by the church to conduct this special service. As Bishop, his calendar was usually full of invitations. Every week was a different church; and a different temptation for Tricia. Like most teenagers, she battled with controlling her sexual desires from the time she hit puberty. "You must wait until you are married" she was told. Most girls in these small islands lost their virginity around the age of fourteen or fifteen. But knowing that that was not the life God wanted for her, Tricia held back. Being an only child, Tricia had no one to talk to about the yearnings she felt. Talking about sex in her house was forbidden. It was almost as if the word and the act was the nastiest thing that ever existed. She cried herself to sleep many nights longing to be touched while not fully understanding what her body was going through. She fought the urges that encompassed her as she listened to her friends reminisce about their many adventures. Tricia could only imagine. Once, she tried to broach the topic with her mother; trying to get a better understanding of the true purpose of sex. Her mother had hit the roof. She banished her then fifteen year old daughter from ever bringing up the topic again. Sex was for adults she hissed, and Tricia was far from needing to know anything about it. It was a mistake most island parents made. Most never took the time to properly educate their children about the wonders and dangers of sex; often leaving them to explore for themselves. She then started to treat sex as an educational topic and found herself researching the different things she heard her friends talking about. Being unable to join in these conversations, Tricia usually retreated to her room at night and would scope the internet to find out just what was going on in the outside world. It was the only form of education she could indulge in without losing her virginity. The things she found stunned her; it was also enticing. The fruit of her searches ranged from hot steamy kisses which lead to passionate love making, to bondage, dominance, sadism and masochism. Tricia spent many nights diving into different theories on sex and often time wondered when she would be able to enjoy these seeming pleasures. She had even watched several pornography movies which often left her body in a weakened state. Without realizing, Tricia had become addicted and a slave to the thought of sex.

Straining to refocus on the service at hand, Tricia glanced around the congregation. She always felt out of sorts sitting at the front of the church, knowing full well that her mind was anywhere else but on God's word. Many services found Tricia longing to feel or taste some unsuspecting congregant. She would quickly assess which male in the congregation may be able to sex her like the wild animal she was. Of course she would never touch a local man. It would have been too risky. These urges heightened with the lack of intimacy in her own marriage.

Currently, she was battling with her love for bondage. The thought of being forced to submit to her partner always got her wet. Having heard of this type of sex in her younger days, she had once discussed the possibility of this with her husband. Being the frank woman that she was, many times Tricia had asked her husband to please her in this manner; much to his dismay. The last time she mentioned it he had jumped out of their bed, got on his knees and started to pray for her soul. Tricia had been utterly disappointed. She had hoped that marriage would have presented her with the opportunity to finally experience all of the things she had longed to engage in; with her partner sent by God. But this was not the case. She resorted to watching others enjoy themselves when her husband had long gone to sleep. She was hooked- and trapped in a sexually boring marriage.

When Elias had proposed to Tricia she had been elated. They had spent three solid years courting and he truly was a gentleman. At the age of 25, and still a virgin, she was a rare catch and Elias thought he had waited long enough to hook his bride. They often times spoken about building a family, and he was quite fascinated by the thought. Tricia shared her longing to be in God's kingdom as her reason for staying a virgin until she tied the knot. So Elias, true to his word, proposed to Tricia soon after he graduated from Codrington College, Barbados' training college for priests. Mere 27 years old himself, Elias was never one to mingle with the wrong crowds. Like Tricia, he knew from early that he wanted to serve God and kept on a straight and narrow path. Having attended an all-boys school, sex was usually far from Elias' mind. He knew about it of course, and he knew some of his colleagues participated in it, but he had a higher calling; one that meant more to him than ten minutes in bed with a woman. As such, Elias kept to himself; always dreaming about the day he would unite with his woman and make her his wife.

On her wedding day, Tricia was ecstatic. Her lily white gown trailed some five feet behind her trim figure. It had been a very private affair in a small cosy garden. They opted to keep this union away from the limelight because of his profession. Everyone thought they should be invited to their priest's wedding. But this wasn't a church service; it was the joining of two very excited but private individuals. The reception had been lively. The dancing and singing made for a joyous occasion. The grounds littered with the natural fauna of the garden, Tricia and Elias took many memorable photos there. Soon, it was time for the couple to head off to their room as the new Mr. and Mrs. Elias Dessington. Tricia couldn't wait. She had always imagined how this night would be. All of her reading and researching would finally come to a head. Her juices started to ooze at the thought of it alone. Hot and steamy were the two words that played over and over in Tricia's mind. Upon reaching their room, she lit several candles. The mood had to be right. The temperature had to be right. She quickly ran a warm bath for the both of them. Filling the tub to just the right level, Tricia poured a generous amount of bubble bath into the water. The foam thickened as she ran her hand back and forth to create just the right effect. While Elias undressed, Tricia poured two glasses of red wine. They both enjoyed the taste of a good Chilean wine. As her husband entered the master bathroom, Tricia requested that he unzip her gown. She felt the desire swell in her as his hands gently removed her clothing to reveal her sexy under garments. After fully undressing, they both enjoyed the warmth of the bath for a bit as they recounted the evening's ceremonies. Playfully leaning into each other, they sipped on their wine and shared some precious moments. "Enough of this" thought Tricia. She kissed her husband passionately. The bubbles rose between the couple and covered every inch of their naked bodies. Elias longed for his beautiful wife. He ravished her lips as she gyrated and wined her waist on his lower region. Not yet. She had wanted this moment to be perfect. Elias climbed out of the tub now and lifted his bride to their bed. There, he gently towelled her damp skin and left a trail of kisses behind the path of his hands. Tricia moaned under his touch. She didn't know what would come next but she was eager to find out. She longed to feel his tongue running over her body; taking advantage of her soft flesh. She moaned again in anticipation. She had imagined Elias torturing her; squeezing and licking her until she exploded from the excitement. Soon, Elias jumped onto the bed with Tricia. He continued kissing her as he positioned himself over her body. Tricia welcomed him by locking his waist between her legs; his firm manhood now rubbing against her sweet dew. Unable to bear it any longer, Elias lined himself up and gently slid into Tricia. She was tight. She was wet. There was a slight pain as Elias moved in and out slowly. Tricia was confused. She didn't think they would be here just yet. "Hold on Elias..." she whispered; but it was too late. By the tenth stroke Elias had exploded in her. It was too much for him to handle; his first piece of the pie. Slowly he rolled off of Tricia, leaving her wondering what on God's green earth had just happened. This wasn't what she had envisioned her first encounter to be like. It was nothing like what she read in the novels. Nothing like what her girlfriends had conveyed. What the hell was that?! Soon she heard a soft snore coming from the direction where Elias had rolled. He lay fast asleep with a look of contentment on his face. Tricia was horrified. "Ok. So we both had a long day, maybe he was just tired" she assured herself. She forced herself to settle down and go to bed, deciding that better must be on the horizon.

CHAPTER 2

It was time for the offertory hymn. Tricia shook that miserable experience from her mind as she stood to partake in the song worship. She loved to sing. From a child she found herself in every choir that she could manage. And they all clamoured after her beautiful voice. The ushers came around to begin the proceedings and Tricia belted the tune of the hymn in solemn appreciation. She always told people, "I am not good at praying, but give me a tune and I will show you how I praise the Lord". True to her word, Tricia sang with rich depth. Her vocal cords, accustomed to the abuse, stretched according to the chords sung by the Calvary gem. Mr Bradshaw smiled at Tricia. He sat two spaces down from her on the same pew. Braddy, as he was affectionately called, always made Tricia cringe. He was a much older man that liked his meat young. For a long time he had been after Tricia but she wouldn't give him the time of day. Braddy always made sure he got close to Tricia whenever the Bishop was scheduled to preach at the church. He figured that one day she would 'give the ole man a break'. Tricia returned the smile politely; trying not to cause any friction between her and any church members. Tricia secretly wondered if maybe he was the culprit that threatened to "out her if she did not repent and change her ways." Looking at the kinky old man, she doubted that.

Like many others in the church, Braddy had his ways. He was one thirsty character. He grew up in the era where any woman was game. Dedication to one woman was a joke. His wife left him after many bouts of infidelity but that didn't stop Braddy. He and another partner of his opened a private "business"; much like the ones Tricia engaged whenever

8

she travelled on church business. Since the island was small, they had had to be very careful with structuring this business. He was a man that liked sex, and he knew many women out there who would want to engage in wild activities, but, because they didn't want to be known, they kept to themselves. He and his partner decided to relieve themselves and give these women what they wanted; needed even. For a hefty fee you could reserve the services of either man. They had recruited a few other men of like ilk to offer variety. A private webpage had been created as the face of the business. No-one knew the men behind the company, and the men didn't know their clients. Once you indicated an interest via email, you were contacted and told the terms of the meeting before anything could occur. You would think that such an operation would have been shut down long time but this was not the case. Braddy knew people in high places, therefore, when the police conducted a sting operation to try to shut down this business, Braddy had called one of his good friends, the Chief of Police of the Eastern Caribbean who immediately "lost" any evidence related to the case. After that close encounter, the owners of the enterprise heightened cyber security and raised their prices exorbitantly. If you wanted their services, you had to pay big bucks as the risk was too great.

In a way, Tricia owed her secret escapades to Braddy. She was one of the few people who knew about it as he had tried to entice her one too many times. In a bout of anger one day, he had let her know he didn't need sex from the likes of her as he had a thriving sex business and had clients from as far as the Middle East. Only once before had she heard about the business. It wasn't known to the average Joe. Braddy and his partner had only set it up for international clientele, and word got around in the well-off societies around the world. After all, most wealthy women knew each other; and each other's boring sex stories. Soon, private jets became a regular sight at the Maurice Bishop Airport. The current government taking the credit for the increase in arrivals of the high end tourist; none the wiser to the real reason these jets made their way to the Spice Isle. Mrs. Bovell, the wife of the former Governor of Calvary Isle, had once approached Tricia about this establishment. She and Tricia roamed the same circles and the middle aged woman had favoured Tricia's friendship. She had heard about it from a close friend who lived in China and had wanted to know if Tricia had any clue who was behind it. Tricia hadn't. One thing was certain, Calvary Isle and

Grenada citizens were not welcomed. Mrs. Bovell told Tricia she sent in a request on the website indicating her interest, but the request was refused. The risk was too great she was told and she had been directed then to a similar business in Canada where she could relieve herself in the same manner without being caught. It was during this conversation that Tricia realized that these businesses dotted across the globe. While she wasn't much of the talker, she had encouraged Mrs. Bovell to tell her more about her adventure; which the woman gladly did. She made Tricia swear to secrecy and she quickly got on to describing her life changing sexual encounters. "The best part Tricia", she prattled on, "is that no one knows you, and no one cares. No attachments necessary and you get what you ask for and much much more". Mrs. Bovell went on to explain that her own sex life had left a lot to be desired and she had thought it best to seek attention elsewhere. Her husband died some five years previously, but her pot didn't stop bubbling. Being the high profile individual she was Mrs. Bovell had refrained from finding another partner to replace her deceased husband. This would not have gone down well with the mostly Christian society even though he no longer served them in office. As such, she had resorted to finding the best solution where the country didn't know about her insatiable thirst. Tricia found out that this was "a thing" with high society and wealthy wives; paying for sexual services that their husbands couldn't or wouldn't perform. It allowed these women to live out their wildest fantasies; many enjoying things they never would have imagined. This piqued Tricia's interest. She let the woman relieve as much information as she could without seeming too interested. After all, her husband was still alive and well so this was merely a conversation for informational purposes.

When Tricia's guest left their usual Saturday tea date, Tricia quickly got to work looking for these businesses online. Surprisingly, they were more "private male services" businesses than Tricia had imagined. It was as if the sex was now more profitable than fast food franchises. Tricia carefully went through the various websites that popped up, taking care to stick close to the ones her friend mentioned as "dependable". She soon had a trip coming up and she thought that maybe she should give it a try; just one time couldn't hurt.

That was the beginning of the end for Tricia. She had boldly booked the services of Raymond for her trip to California. Having gone through the rigorous process, she finally paid half of the $10, 000 US fee for the six hours she was entitled to. Luckily, it wasn't money that her husband would have easily missed. While Anglican salaries were the bottom of the religious barrel, Tricia had been left 2 hefty insurance policies when her mother and father had passed away in the car accident. In addition, there was a massive pay out from the company responsible for the crash. Their driver had been driving under the influence and flew right out of a red stop light; knocking her parents' car into an upcoming natural rock formation. Their deaths shook Calvary. Many still mourned some 3 years later.

Thinking about her parents always left Tricia with mixed emotions. She loved those two dearly. But she did believe they sheltered her too much. Tricia had only really been able to experience life after she met Elias when she was 22 years old. Even then, she was placed on a curfew and only permitted to go to certain places with him. "No one is going to think my girl child is a wildling" her father would sternly suggest. "Young man, return my daughter by 10:30 PM or that is the last you will be seeing of her!" This was daddy's chime each and every date Tricia had gone on with Elias. And true to his word, Elias always returned her right on time. One night, they had gone to watch a movie which would have ended well past her curfew. Tricia had been adamant she was not leaving until the end. Elias, scared out of his wits, left Tricia in the safety of the cinema and ran 2 blocks to her home to explain the situation to her father. "Sir, short of dragging Tricia out of there, she has refused to leave and I don't want to disobey your request" Elias stressed. Ray Callendar had been amused at the young man's respect for him. He chased him away stating that his wife had demanded only hours earlier that he let go of his reigns on Tricia. As much as Tricia's dad was the man of the house, he listened to his wife. He believed it was the security of a long and happy marriage. Relieved, Elias returned to his girlfriend's side. Tricia was a bit uncomfortable being left alone, but she figured he would have returned at some point. Without a word between the two, they settled to watch the rest of the movie.

That situation plus many more made Tricia begin to put down her foot with her parents. She wanted to grow and explore life without being hovered over like some sick puppy. It was only then that she could learn to be a woman; learn about whom she truly was and what she wanted in life. Tricia wanted to spread her wings.

11

CHAPTER 3

Before the death of her parents, Tricia honestly believed they probably would have had sex once; when she was conceived. She cannot remember any loving touches or caresses that may have passed between her dad and his wife. As such, a hidden treasure came as a total shock to her when she had embarked on clearing out their home to start the renovations. While she kept many memoirs of the two, the old house was on its last legs. Tricia's parents loved simplicity. They both hated the thought of moving out in order for someone to come and spruce up the place. It was a house that her father built with his own hands. When Ray Callendar approached his wife's father to ask for her hand in marriage, the old man had asked him "and where exactly do you propose to lay her head?" The question was valid. While Ray knew Andrea was the only woman for him, he didn't think about where they would live when they got married. He then quickly set out to build them a home. His own father had left some land for him when he had died and he figured that would be the perfect place to start his own family. He garnered the help of his closest friend who was a draughtsman by profession. After completing the design, he set about purchasing the necessary materials to build what he hoped would be their future home.

Andrea had had no clue what he was up to. He told her he was busy working on a project and he would be unavailable for a few days. This was no surprise to her as he had little projects ever so often, so she gave him his space. Ray toiled day and night to build that little chattel house. He refused any further help from anyone. This was supposed to be his gift to his wife; if she accepted the offer. On completion, Ray painted the chattel house in

Andrea's favourite colours; peach trimmed with brown. She loved earth tone colours. Even the clothes she wore always had an earthy feel to them; close to nature. Once he was satisfied with his project, Ray approached Andrea's father once again. He kindly asked the man to accompany him to the place where he intended for them to call home. Mr. Kirton gladly obliged him. When he reached the lot which boasted of a spanking new home, the man was touched. One of his good friends, Andrea's godfather, had been watching over the project from afar. He told the good gentleman about Ray's intentions and he had promised to keep an eye out for him. So Mr. Kirton knew about the house before Ray had even completed it. However, what stood before him had surpassed his imagination. When his friend had told him Ray worked hard to build that house, he hadn't expected much. What justice can one man do alone? But the sight that stood before him told him that he was about to place his daughter in good hands.

The house was medium sized. It had three bedrooms and one bathroom. It was made of durable Purple Heart wood and the bathroom and kitchen were made of wall. Ray turned that concrete with nothing but a shovel and a strong back. He lay brick by brick for the foundation and even built up the side walls by himself. He took great care to reinforce the bricks with steel and concrete to prevent any cracks from surfacing. The wooden bits he slaved over as Purple Heart was a strong wood. It bent several of the nails he had tried to hammer in but Ray wouldn't give up. He got bigger nails and used greater force to drive them in. Ray was a man that believed in hard work; his pride encompassed being able to accomplish things for himself in life.

By the time he completed the tour with Mr. Kirton, the man was nodding profusely. "She is all yours once she accepts young man. You have outdone yourself and I am well pleased." Ray popped the question that night after he took her to dinner. In that time, it was rare to eat out as it was frightfully expensive. When Ray told Andrea they would be having dinner at the local Hilton hotel, she had been taken aback. She racked her brain trying to think about what the special occasion could have been for such an expensive feast. Marriage was the last thing on her mind as they were still yet young. She always wanted a family of her own but she had figured that would happen later in life; not at age 20. However, they had a wonderful dinner and Ray formally asked Andrea for her hand in marriage. She was thrilled. Jumping for joy she readily accepted; then her concerns grew. Shortly after placing the engagement ring on her finger, Ray was saddled with a string of questions. He smiled gently and returned every response with renewed confidence. She was to finish her education before she even thought about having children. They would be very careful not to slip up. But in the event that a child was conceived, they agreed they would keep it and work it out. Tricia was indeed born during Andrea's last year in university. Her mother delivered her and got right back to work; fighting to complete her degree. Ray took care of Tricia in the early days, but then sent her off to nursery soon after. He worked hard to provide for his family. A carpenter by profession, her dad worked on many projects ranging from new homes to extensions on existing structures. He made certain his wife and his daughter wanted for nothing.

Pondering now how difficult it must have been to toil in the sun all day and come home to a bubbling baby girl at night, Tricia appreciated what her father had sacrificed for her. She reverently managed the dismantling of the old house; careful to take lots of pictures for the capsule she had wanted to compile for the place. It had outlived its usefulness. By the time her parents passed away, the only thing left to do was to rebuild. While she wasn't planning on selling the property, she had decided she would rent it out. While dismantling the old building, the contractor had called her for an item which they found just a foot below the floor boards. It was an old chest and they figured she may want to add it to her collectables. Tricia took one look at the stuffy chest and decided she didn't have any use for it. But why was it placed under the house? She decided she would take some time to go through it later. Instead of leaving it to be hauled away with the rest of the rubble, Tricia asked the work men to place the old trunk in the back of her jeep.

When Tricia arrived home later that night, she decided it would be a good time to go through the contents of the trunk. Her husband was attending a diocesan meeting so she would be alone for at least a couple hours. She carefully took in the intricate details of the chest. It wasn't just any old chest. It was carved mahogany wood that had seen some better days. The clasp and lock were made of pure gold indicating a rich existence. The Victorian design on the chest boasted of embellished hand carvings; showing the artistic beauty as foreseen by its craftsman. Tricia took a clean damp cloth and began to wipe the grime from the chest. "This could be worth a few pennies at an auction" she mused to herself. As she rotated the glorified box, items on the inside shifted. They hadn't found a key at the work site so she had no clue how to open it. Inspecting the lock a bit more closely, Tricia figured she would be able to unscrew the latch. Hunting for her husband's tool box, she got to work on the 2 by 5 foot mahogany chest. Within half an hour, Tricia had managed to remove both parts to the lock. When she opened it, she was not prepared for what she saw.

The contents peered at Tricia in sheer glory, as if wondering why they had been left alone for so long. Tricia passed her hand over the items in awe. The chest had more than one compartment. The top tray contained a mix of sex toys; artistically made. Each item had had its own section in the tray which ensured nothing got mixed up or lost. Tricia's eyes took in the beauty of each piece. They had almost looked as if they were specially made for their owner. The quality was not sweat shop grade, but boasted of a lushness accompanied by intricate detail.

"What was that box doing under my parents' house" she wondered. Gently, Tricia removed the first item. It had looked like someone had chopped the penis off of a very well-endowed man. However, this was no ordinary dildo. It was about 9 inches in length she approximated. The material felt smooth to the touch; almost looked like glass. On careful inspection, Tricia realized it was actually an opaque pink crystal. It was magnificent! The dildo had a thick girth. The shaft had several artificial ridges which resembled the veins of a real penis. Just the sight of this item caused a wetness in Tricia's undies. After running her hand over the item several times, she gently replaced in onto its velvety bed. Beside that lay another crystal toy. This one had a different shape. It had a cone like shaft which widened to the middle of it, then tapered off to a standing stem. Tricia recognised this as a butt plug. This too had special groves that made Tricia wonder about the immense pleasure the toy must have brought to its owner. Beside this lay a small bottle labelled 'LUBE'. Soon, she also returned this item to its rightful place in the tray. The rest of the tray held other pleasurable goodies. Anal beads, a g-spot vibrator, 2 bullets of differing sizes, clit stimulators and ben wa balls to name a few. There was another compartment which held a whip, handcuffs, feathers, different scented massage oils and many other items. The box was a wealth of hot sexual pleasures.

Confused, Tricia closed the chest and sat trying to figure out what it all meant. Nothing in there seemed to belong to a man. It was all female sex toys she had believed. But what did it all mean? Her mother wouldn't even talk to her about sex so these things couldn't belong to her...could they? As Tricia tried to come to grips with the container in front of her, she noticed a tiny indentation to the bottom of the chest. It looked as if there was a secret drawer there. Searching, she was unable to locate a latch for the drawer. Tricia then tried to apply slight pressure and the two inch tall drawer popped right out. In it, there were several pieces of paper which looked like letters. Each one held a different date; all in her mother's hand writing.

Three hours had passed before Tricia heard Elias's vehicle pull into their garage. She had been so enthralled by what was written in those letters that the time slipped by. Quickly, she arose and put everything back in its place. She hid the chest in her portion of the closet beneath some blankets, planning to return to it as soon as possible.

"Hi honey," her husband chimed cheerfully. "How was your day?"

Tricia leaned over to receive the daily kiss that her husband planted on her forehead. He was such a loving gentleman.

"Today was interesting," she replied. She went on to tell Elias about the demolition of the house and where the contractors were at. She withheld all information about her new found treasure. Not sure how to grapple with what she had seen herself, Tricia needed a bit more time to digest it all.

Elias then began to tell Tricia about the meeting he had just attended. This recollection was not as boring as previous ones, but Tricia was immensely distracted. Her mind was now on the contents of the letters she read. It was almost as if her mother had written a diary of sexual desires to her husband, but never delivered the letters. They spoke of fear. Fear of being judged for her wants and needs. Fear of being rejected by the one she loved. Her mother wrote about the things she wanted to do and feel, with her husband. It was an intimacy that lacked in their marriage and this was her way of venting. Soon, after several letters, Tricia realized how sad and depressed her mother had actually been. Writing these letters was her way of coping with her feelings. She wrote of being the best wife she could be. Giving her husband the best life she could. She had washed and cleaned, cooked and ironed. She kept the finances in order and paid the bills, never spending a solitary stray cent. Then there was the difficulty of raising a decent child in this day and age. However, Mrs. Callendar never received the gratitude that she had longed for. Many nights, Mr. Callendar had come home tired from a long day at work. He usually would come in and go directly to the bathroom. About half an hour later he would emerge clean and relieved of the stresses of his day. By then, Andrea had his food laid out for him on the table. His cutlery all in the right places. He always started with his appetizer, then his main, and a cup of coffee to complete. Ray wasn't much for desert. During this time Tricia would have been already preparing herself for bed, as she and her mother would have had their dinner earlier. On completion of his meal, Mr. Callendar would retreat to their bedroom, never to be seen again until the morning. Tricia never knew what went on in there after that. She seldom ventured into her parents' bedroom, especially at night. But from reading her mother's letters, it appeared as if nothing much transpired. Her mother pined about longing to be touched; wanting to feel love and affection. She had apparently purchased these items throughout the years, but had never even so much as used them. She respected her husband and had wanted him to be the one to make love to her; not she to herself. The purchases served as a pacifier for the woman who dared not tell her husband how she truly felt. She spoke of the naughty things that passed through her mind; of the urges that she felt daily to be held and delighted. The letters detailed how she cried herself to sleep many nights after her husband had long gone to sleep. It had been torture.

Tricia now felt a pang of depression for her mother. Thinking back, she had indeed been a good woman to her dad. The least he could have done was given her the pleasure she had desired. Tricia now felt closer to her mother than ever before. Thinking about her own situation with the lack of intimacy in her marriage, Tricia now felt to reach out beyond the grave and hug her mother. One of the letters had said that she had hoped her daughter would never be in this 'place' and if she did find herself there that she would have the courage to get out. "Get out and run my child" the words read, as if she had been speaking directly to Tricia. At that point, Tricia made a decision. She would reach out to her husband one more time, but if that failed, she would take matters into her own hands.

Chapter 4

Some 3 years later, Tricia was well seasoned in her extra curricula activities. Her attempt to get Elias to open up sexually had failed miserably. She had gone back and completed reading the letters, then hid the box in a special location on her parents' now rented property. Later that week, Tricia put on a set of the sexiest lingerie she owned. She usually kept these things hidden from her husband; merely making purchases to satisfy herself. The red lace and satin pieces revealed much of her plush curves. She had scented the bedroom with a touch of lavender. The music was at a good pitch and the room was dim. The setting was just right for some serious love making. It is not something that they engaged in often, and when they did, it was awful. Elias would hop on and back off without Tricia so much as breaking a sweat. Tonight was to be different. Tonight she wanted to take the lead. She laid out some oil to give her husband an erotic massage. Nothing on his body would go untouched. Tonight he was going to find out what some good head felt like. She had planned to suck the life out of him. The only way he would understand her desires is if she showed him exactly how she wanted to be loved.

That night, Elias returned home from a service. Tricia had made up some excuse as to why she couldn't attend so that she could prepare properly. As soon as he exited the bathroom after relieving himself of his clothing, Tricia led him to the dining table. Sitting in bare short pants, Elias hungrily asked what was for dinner; Tricia replied "me". With that she sat on the edge of the table before him. Her silky house robe now wide opened revealed the risky outfit that she wore beneath. Elias nearly choked on his tongue. He had never seen his wife like this before. Tricia didn't hesitate any further.

"Eat me Elias, taste me..." her voice trailed as she gyrated on the table in front of her husband. Her long hair fell over her shoulders, barely covering the plump flesh of her breast that protruded over her half cup bra. Elias found his voice.

"What the hell are you doing Tricia? Please put on some clothes!" Tricia refused to be deterred. More determined than ever, Tricia jumped off the table as her husband arose and shoved back the chair. In one fluid movement she had gone on her knees and grabbed hold of her husband's penis. Her long hands groped his groin as she ripped at his pants to get it off. By this time Elias was all but running from his wife. He hadn't wanted to hurt her but he had never seen her like this before and it was well beyond his imagination. Tricia successfully managed to drag his pants to his knees in the middle of the struggle; her womanhood now oily from the thought of what she was about to do. The entire episode gave her a life that she had never dared to experience; she demanded what was hers. With grace she placed his penis in her mouth; hoping that it would weaken her prey. On the contrary. Elias yelped at the sight of his wife performing these nasty acts. He was traumatised. Never had he imagine his wife even knew about these sexual performances furthermore to be able to execute them so well. He pushed Tricia off with a bit too much force and she bumped her head onto the edge of the table. Once he realized she was ok, he hastily retreated to the bedroom. Tricia smiled. He would be cornered by the stage of romance. Elias paused at the sight of their room. It was almost dark, and there was a faint scent coming from the four corners. Soon Tricia was behind him. She reached around his body and pinched his nipples. This startled Elias. He turned to face his wife with a look of stark puzzlement. Tricia didn't falter. She placed her hands around his waist and flicked her tongue over his nipples. Elias didn't know what to make of it all. Again, he pushed Tricia away from him and slowly stepped backwards into the room. The chase ignited excitement in Tricia as she bounded forward and knocked Elias straight onto his back on their bed. Hungrily she licked and sucked the curve of his neck. Her nails dug deep in his back as she willed him to feel her desire for him. By this time her panties had been completely soaked through. Tricia paused long enough to sit on Elias' face. His glasses cocked to one side as she lined up her lips with his own. After a few seconds and realizing he was not returning the lust for her body, Tricia had stopped. Peering into her husband's eyes, she watched as a single tear flowed down the side of his face. He had looked as if a burglar had entered the house and had placed a gun to his head; the fear was real. Tricia now climbed off of her husband.

"What is it Elias? Are you not attracted to me?" Tricia could feel the tears forming in her own eyes. Most men literally fell all over her. Some bold enough to tell her their desires, others just showed their gratitude with an appreciative glance. She just could not understand her own husband's lack of intimacy.

Elias peered at his distraught wife. It wasn't that he didn't love her. And it certainly wasn't that he wasn't attracted to her. He just was never exposed to this level of affection. As far as he was concerned, only porn stars and whores behaved in this manner. Not respectable adults, and certainly not the Bishop and his wife! Elias quickly expressed his disgust to Tricia.

"I don't know what has gotten into you, but I think you need to prayer about this," came his reprimand. "I don't ever want to see you behaving in this manner again!"

Tricia was dumbfounded. Her own husband, the one whom she gave her life to, had rejected her. She was left riddled with sorrow. That night, she took an ice cold bath and slept on the couch. Elias hadn't come for her. He was still reeling at what had unfolded only moment s before. How could she expect a Bishop to behave in that manner? He had planned on going on a fast and praying for her deliverance. Clearly the devil was at work in trying to uproot his marriage, but he wouldn't let him get the upper hand. On the third night sleeping on their couch, Elias pleaded with Tricia to return to their bed. She had hardly spoken a word to him over those days and just opted to cry. Tricia, figuring they might have been a glimmer of hope at that point, agreed to re-join him. Unfortunately that was not to be. No sooner had Elias mounted her, had he gone into the same old boring routine. With that, Tricia vowed not to die a miserable undersexed woman as her mother had.

CHAPTER 5

It was soon time for communion. Before they got around to this, there were confessionary prayers. Her husband led the congregation with the words from 1 John chapter 1, verses 8 and 9:

"If we say we have no sin, we deceive ourselves and the truth is not in us. If we confess our sins, God is faithful and just and will forgive our sins and cleanse us from all unrighteousness. Let us therefore confess our sins..."

Using the red Book of Common Prayer, the congregation responded:

"Almighty God and Heavenly Father, we have sinned against you and one another. In thought, word and deed. And in what we have left undone. We are sorry and repent of all our sins. Forgive us all that has passed, and grant that we may serve you in the newness of life to the Glory of your name. Amen."

The Bishop then followed with the Prayer of Absolution: "Almighty God have mercy on you, and forgive you all your sins through our Lord Jesus Christ, strengthen you in all goodness, and by the power of the Holy Spirit keep you in eternal life. Amen."

Confessions. Tricia had racked up quite a bit of those over the years. Her heart felt heavy again; she felt like she was a total disappointment to God. But what was she to do? How do you suppress these types of feelings? Tricia decided she would join the congregation for communion. She rose from her seat as the usher indicated that her pew should be the first to go. Ever since that fateful night Tricia had stayed away from the Lord's altar. On her way up, something caught her eye. Roger Duncan genuflected. His bright red robe hung loosely over his tall stately frame.

Tricia had known him from school days; they were good friends at one point in time. Roger had been one of those boys that all the girls wanted to be with; and he obliged them all. As a teenager Roger was known for his stamina. He held the record for bedding the most girls in one week. Now to see Roger adorning the altar of the Lord brought a smile to Tricia's face. He had adored her at school, but she was the only woman that turned him down. Every time Roger saw Tricia, he would try to engage her in the possibility of making her wildest dreams come true, but Tricia would have none of it. He definitely was attractive, but she was scared; scared of the wrath of her parents; scared of the wrath of God. But Roger never backed down. He had finally become her very first sin. When he had heard she was engaged to Elias he had been furious. He had always wanted to claim her as his own; to make her his wife. Roger knew she was still a virgin. No man could ever relay the story of picking Tricia's cherry and he wanted that honour.

Roger's eyes connected with Tricia's now. A smile escaped his lips as he glanced over her soft delicate hair. Curls hung loosely from the sides of her head. Roger imagined himself grabbing those curls as he slid deep into her throat. Shaking his head feverishly, Roger quickly turned back to the task at hand. He was trying to be a changed man. On his mother's dying bed she had pleaded with him to give up his whoring ways. Turn himself over to God and ask for forgiveness of his sins. Roger loved no one like he loved his mother. He would have gladly exchanged her cancer filled body for his own just so she wouldn't die. But alas, that could not be. His mother's death had been the lowest point in his life. The product of a fatherless home, Mrs. Duncan had raised her only child the best way she could. His father's infidelities had been no secret in the small islands. Any woman that moved Dennis Duncan had sex with. He was what was known as 'the village ram'. And he held that title proudly 'til death. Roger, having not had the guidance of a grounded father, grew up rebellious. His way of coping with the void in his life was to 'juck down' everything that would let him through. His conquests ranged from girls his own age, to a couple teachers at his school and even a few grandmothers in the district. He was a terror and then some. But the women loved him. He had a soft sweet demeanour. If you had seen him for the first time, you would have never guessed the acts this young man could get himself up to.

Tricia now gracefully passed Roger on the way up to the altar. He politely nodded and she humbly returned the favour. Tricia could smell his cologne as they passed each other. It was strongly scented and full of spice. He had almost gotten his way with her in a moment of weakness; almost. If there was one man from the islands that could get Tricia Dessington to cheat on her husband, it would have been Roger. As Tricia knelt by the altar to receive her body and blood, she felt overwhelmed with grief. After Elias had rejected her advances, she had dived right into a stream of infidelity. More often than not she travelled alone to cover the many appearance requests that she and her husband usually received. They were so many that they usually had to split up in order to meet just half of them. Her ministry took her to Nigeria, Italy, Hong Kong and Singapore to name a few. And each time she travelled, Tricia booked herself a play date as she affectionately called them. She felt his eyes on her before she rose from her position. She could tell Roger had been boring holes in her ass. Secretly, she had wanted to call him and ask him to do her a favour, but she held strain. He was more than qualified for the job, but he was too close to home even though he didn't live on island anymore. She couldn't let the locals know of her activities now could she? It would be too much of a risk and she couldn't be slack about these things. She knew very well that Roger had wanted to marry her. She couldn't afford to lead him on now as she was a married woman. Besides, he had now given his life over to God. It didn't make any sense both of them going to hell because of her.

Roger sighed heavily. He had fought the entire morning not to let the thought of Tricia Dessington cloud his mind. It had been futile. Whenever she sang chills ran through his body. She was indeed a beautiful song bird. Roger imagined pounding those vocal chords with his penis. There was something different about Tricia now. She seemed to have a glow about her. He had wondered how her husband had been treating her. Everything that glitters is not gold, and he was certain he could do a better job as her man; as her husband. His mother had been disappointed that he hadn't cleaned up his ways earlier and "tried to hook a wife like Tricia." She had been fascinated by the woman and often jaded Roger about trying to win her heart. "She would be great for you honey," his mother often chimed. "Just show her what a gentleman you could be." His mother knew oh too well that he had a little space in Tricia's heart.

The young girl used to encourage Roger to come to church with her and participate in the different church activities. Unfortunately, Roger in his young ignorance had used these events as his stomping ground. Word usually got back to Tricia about the activities he got himself up to and she used to heavily chastise him. Roger never took heed. He was having too much fun. The decent life was boring. He had also figured that since he was following in his dad's footsteps, maybe the man would return and be a father to him. At least they would have something in common. It was a twisted mentality, but Roger had known no better. It was the only way he knew how to reach out to his dad; hoping for a relationship which never came to light.

Roger usually ignored his mother's words; he would have none of it. Tricia had rejected him too many times clearly she wasn't interested in him; but that made him want her even more. Granted, his reputation wasn't one that exactly screamed "you are my one and only" but he knew what he had felt in his heart for Tricia. She was different. He didn't just want to fuck her; he wanted to make love to her. Make her his queen; and then fuck her like no other. He was quite certain that had she given him the time of day he would have already changed his ways. He also told her as much. One night after choir practise, Roger had been on his way to one of his girl's house. He saw Tricia walking alone on her way home so he pulled up and offered her a ride. There was reluctance on her face, but Roger swore to her he would be a gentleman. After the last story had reached Tricia, she had had enough. She was barely speaking to Roger and he knew then that she did have feelings for him; else why would she care what he did? Swinging the truck around from the direction he had originally been going in, Roger got out and opened the door for Tricia to take a seat. She did so without much fuss and thanked him for his kindness. Her house was some 3 miles away and it would have taken her quite some time to walk there. Soon they were in deep conversation and naturally it led to Tricia asking Roger when he had planned to give up his current escapades and be a real man. Roger had been offended.

"I give the women what they want babes. It is them that need to leave me alone!" Roger smirked at Tricia now. He proceeded to ask her how things were going for her 'down below' and if she had needed any help. He kissed her hand affectionately and she blushed uncontrollably. She was more than curious about sex, but she dared not try anything at that point. Roger saw a glistening in Tricia's eyes. He placed his hand on her leg and reassured her he would be as gentle or as rough as she needed him to be. He could feel her weaken to his touch.

"Do you want me to show you a few things baby? You know you have a special place in my heart…" Tricia took a deep breath. She had indeed heard of the many things Roger could do with his tongue; things she only ever read about. He could show her much more than a few things and Tricia knew that; it was what she had feared. Roger veered off course now onto a deserted path.

"Where are you taking me Roger?" Tricia asked.

"Don't be scared" Roger replied. Soon, he brought the truck to a stop. They were surrounded by darkness and Tricia had been nervous. Calvary Isle was as safe as it got. There were hardly any muggings furthermore murders so she was generally safe. She could hear Roger breathing heavily in the seat beside her. She heard the sound of his zip becoming undone.

"I don't think this is a good idea Roger" Tricia mumbled. He could feel her energy becoming undone. He knew he had an effect on her, but he didn't want to push his luck. Gently, he took her hand and placed it in his lap. He had pulled his dick out and was guiding her to feel it. Tricia's hand jerked.

"Don't be scared baby; I won't bite if you don't want me to." Roger now replaced her hand onto his dick. In response Tricia grabbed it. It was thick and nice. She could feel the blood flowing through the veins along the shaft. It was warm to the touch. Tricia gasped. Roger guided her hand up and down his penis as he told her of all the things he had wanted to do to her. Tricia melted with each word. Slowly, he turned her head to his, and had kissed her deeply. A powerful tongue traced the inside of her mouth. She returned the favour with as much vigour as a virgin could. It had been her first kiss. She had been longing to be touched and Roger knew just what to do. His free hand roamed to her breast and squeezed. A moan escaped Tricia's mouth. He could feel her nipple begin to pout through her thin top. As a small woman, it wasn't often she needed to wear a bra. Her breasts were firm and complimented her frame beautifully. His hand quickly moved to readjust her seat. He needed full access to her body to treat her the best way he knew how. Tricia's body began to react. Roger quickly unbuttoned her shirt to reveal two luscious plump breasts; her nipples rock hard. His hand roamed under her skirt. Playful fingers squeezed and massaged her inner thigh, on its way up to its final destination. When Roger reached the centre of her core he grabbed it gently. God, she was wet for him. He could feel her feminine dew seeping through her panties.

"Tricia, let me taste you baby." The request caused Tricia to gasp "I can't do this…no we can't do this…" Tricia's breathing was fast and shallow now. She had never felt like this before. Her hips involuntarily wined in the seat to the pulsing rhythm of Roger's squeezing. Roger was pleading with her. He had wanted to please her to the point of no return. She still had his dick in a vice grip; not sure what to do with herself. Tricia arched her body as Roger's fingers probed beneath her panty line. He was searching for her nub. He had managed to get one breast into his mouth and he sucked viciously. Tricia had been moaning and wining now begging for more. Her free hand grabbed a handful of his fluffy hair. It was too much for her body to bear. Soon he found what he had been looking for. Her clit was drowning in the pool that had formed between her legs. Tricia now called his name loudly as she opened up to welcome him.

"Cum for me baby…" Roger placed one finger in the depth of her vagina. She was tight. God he had wanted to fuck her so hard. He moved his finger slowly in and out now. Not wanting to hurt her. Tricia was going mad in the passenger seat. She now grabbed onto her head as the feeling overwhelmed her. One foot had found its way across the driver's seat as Tricia had exposed herself to his touch. Roger caressed and teased her. Not yet. He needed to taste her. He couldn't let her explode just as yet. He moved his body over her to get better access to her feminine flower. Eagerly, positioned his face between her legs now; longing to taste her. Tricia moaned in anticipation. When Roger's tongue landed on his meal, Tricia's body convulsed. He skilfully sucked and licked her until her groans increased. His tongue slid back and forth, in and out of her vagina. Roger was enjoying this just as much as Tricia. Tricia's feet now pressed against the roof of the cabin of the truck. With both hands firmly under her ass, Roger guided his tongue further into the depth of her vagina. It moved quickly now driving its prey to call out his name. Her hips pushed up on his face as she begged him to give her more. Roger gave her exactly what she asked for and more. Soon a pleasant cry escaped Tricia's lips. Roger's face covered with the wetness that now dripped from her pulsing core. He moved in savagely and begged her to let him fuck her; biting and licking her inner thighs on the way up. He wanted her to feel his desire for her. He already knew how she had felt about him. The juices all over his face spoke volumes. He had lost count of the number of times she had cum. She had back to back orgasms as he rocked her to ecstasy. Tricia shook her head. She couldn't just give up her virginity to anyone; especially not Roger and definitely not in the front of a truck in a dark road. That would make her just like the rest. She didn't want to be one of his statistics. Clouded by the events that just occurred, Tricia fought to regain control of her body. She had already gone too far. Roger now had the title of 'First Kiss', 'First Touch 'and 'First Taste'. She definitely couldn't give him the pleasure of the 'First Sex'. Reluctantly Roger backed away. He truly loved Tricia, and he would do anything that she asked of him. When she asked him to stop water sprung to his eyes. Tricia saw them, but she needed to digest what had just occurred. Never before had she been so loose with her actions. These were things that she only heard her friends talking about. How was it that Roger could make her feel this way…and she loved it?

"We can't do this Roger…I can't…" Tricia had mumbled. Roger's body went weak. Tricia must think him an animal. He got up and assisted her in pulling her clothes together.

"I'm sorry" came his soft reply. "I didn't mean to hurt you". Roger could kick himself for what he had just done. While he had wanted to delight Tricia, he didn't want her to hate him. She promised him that she didn't but she needed to compose herself. He had felt much better after he realized she wasn't angry with him. He soon backed out of the side road and proceeded to take her to her home. "I think I'm in love with you Tricia…" She hadn't known what to say to him. She knew he had admired her from a tender age, but he wasn't exactly the type of man Tricia had seen herself settling down with; neither was he the type that she could take home and introduce to her parents. Him rampages across the female population had grown to tremendous heights and Tricia wanted none of it in her life. There was no doubt that Roger knew how to please her and was quite willing; he just wasn't the man she would marry. Tricia got out of the truck without a word. She gave a polite nod and hastily retreated to her home. The tears that had filled Roger's eyes now began their painful trail down his cheek.

CHAPTER 6

Tricia hadn't forgotten the experience. It had been well engraved in her mind actually. Her father had seen the truck pull up and he spent the following two hours talking to his daughter about the dangers of men like Roger.

"They are only out for one thing Tricia" her father had stressed. "Don't let me see you getting mixed up with the likes of that man do you hear me?"

Tricia nodded, knowing her father spoke the truth. Roger Duncan was bad news. There was no one that Tricia could talk to about her urges; no one that could understand just what she had just gone through. It was the reason she was walking home alone that night in the first place. She didn't feel to be around her friends. She always felt like an outcast with them. They partied, they limed and they drank alcohol. They had sex and they enjoyed all the aspects of life that most 19 year olds indulged in. Most times she wondered why people even bothered to be friends with her. She felt like a caged bird in her parents' house; only being able to attend church and school activities. But Tricia also knew that the way of life that God wanted for her meant that she needed to forgo worldly pleasures.

What had just occurred in Roger's truck was far from godly. Tricia felt good; too good. Was this how Adam and Eve felt when they ate of the fruit of the garden? Tricia's eyes were opened now somewhat. Things that had been merely a thought had now become her reality. She fought feverishly that night to forget what had happened but to no avail. Every time it crossed her mind, Tricia's vagina involuntarily became wet. After that night Roger became even wilder than he originally was. He had opened his heart to Tricia, the only woman he had ever loved, and she had rejected him. He felt awful. He had turned around his truck and drove straight to the woman he had first planned on going by. He rinsed her out that night to the point where she said she didn't want to see him for another week. His ego had been busted, and every woman he linked up with after that night had felt his wrath.

Tricia was hurt when she had heard about Roger's subsequent encounters. She felt that maybe he had been willing to change; for her. But that had not been the case. Roger had gotten worst. He didn't know how to manage Tricia's rejection. She hadn't even responded when he had told her he was in love with her. Well the other women loved him, didn't they? Why should he hold up his life for Ms. Goody Two Shoes? Roger vowed to enjoy every woman that passed his way since Tricia Callendar didn't want him. There was no reason now to stop.

Following that night, Tricia went into her shell. The next evening, she came home from rehearsals quite late and went straight to the internet trying to find out more about what had actually happened that previous night. It was her first step over the border and she needed to understand just what she had gotten herself into. The internet is a wealth of knowledge to the unsuspecting teen. She soon found loads of pictures and pornography which detailed her very experience. Graphic as it may have been, Tricia knew nothing about the human body past what she had learnt at school. One website she visited encouraged her to touch herself. Tricia hesitated. Why would she want to touch herself? Was that what God would want her to do? In the world of sex this was called masturbation she had noted. She decided to look a bit further into this and see what it was really all about. Submerging herself into the many sites, Tricia had been introduced to self-pleasuring. "Well since I'm supposed to stay a virgin until I am married, this must be the way that God wants me to preserve myself. She decided to try this masturbation thing. Her parents had long gone to bed so she had ample opportunity to figure it out. One of her favourite pornography movies that she had saved, she decided to watch. She had heard the guys at school saying that a little porn always got them in the mood. All Tricia knew was that whenever she watched a movie, her body reacted the same way; she got wet. Sure enough, ten minutes into the movie she felt her oil start to ooze. Tricia had taken a bath prior to turning on her laptop and she now sat naked in front of her screen. As the movie got into gear, Tricia let her hands begin to explore her body. The man had started to lick the vagina of his partner. He was showing great skill in making her wine and wiggle under his tongue. Tricia immediately remembered the things Roger had done to her. Soon, her mind ventured away from the movie in front of her and back to the events of that fateful night. She had hardly been able to forget the way Roger had made her feel. Both her hands now squeezed her breasts. Her nipples perked and were iron hard. Her breasts themselves were firm. They were indeed beautiful she mused as she looked down at the damage her hands were doing. Intermittently, Tricia plucked each nipple; massaging her soft flesh along the way. This action sent shivers down her spine. She was now imagining Roger feeling her vagina. She lay back on her bed and let one hand venture between her legs. Saying she was horny is an understatement. Tricia recalled how Roger had inserted his finger deep inside her. She tried this, curving the top of her finger in search of what others call the g spot. She was very wet. Soon, Tricia was lost in her own world. She was wining and panting as if a man were there with her. Within a few minutes she climaxed and her body shook with delight.

Before long, her body grew cold. The session had excited her, but the warmth of a human body next to her still didn't exist. Tricia figured it would have to do until she got married. At least she had been able to get an orgasm. It had felt good. It was almost as if she had been back in Roger's truck with him. Her imagination runs wild and deep so it was easy for her to envision this.

These memories once again flooded her as she sat through the end of the service. Tricia had spent many a night since then pleasuring herself. Even after she had married and realized her love life would have left lots to be desired, Tricia had resorted to masturbating… and then, infidelity.

"Mrs. Dessington." His voice sounding deep and mellow. Roger had decided to go over and say hello after the service had ended. It had been a few years since he had seen Tricia face to face. Since his mother's death, Roger had retreated into his own head space. He reflected on the fragility of life and had decided there had to be more to it than fucking these bitches. He recounted his own loss and had even considered that never being able to convince Tricia to be his girl must have been punishment for his lifestyle; it's the only thing he could ever recall wanting more than a relationship with his father. No one had heard from him for a few years. Roger left the island soon after the burial. As an investment analyst, it was easy for him to get a job just about anywhere. By that time the one woman he had loved was long married, his father never so much as gave him the time of day before he himself had passed away. And then he lost his mother. There had been no real reason to stay in Calvary Isle. Even though several of his female companions had pleaded with him to stay and let them take care of him, Roger had had enough. He needed to go where no one knew his name; where he could start over his life.

"Roger!" Tricia exclaimed. She hadn't seen where he had turned after the service had ended. She stared now into his mocha eyes. He was still a captivating man at his age. One could see the maturity etched into his brow which showed stories of worries untold.

"How have you been keeping?" Tricia smiled. She had respected Roger even after what had transpired between them. It was the only scenario that he had never repeated to a soul. Tricia had not just been any woman; she was a queen and he wanted to be her king. While the other women hadn't meant much to him, Tricia was different. Roger never reached out to her again after that night so many years ago. Before he left the island, he had avoided her like the plague. He missed every event that he suspected she would have attended. That wasn't too hard given the tight reign her father had had on the girl. He never could get close enough to have a serious conversation with her. But that night, he had gotten an opportunity; and he had blown it.

"I'm not bad ma'am, and yourself?" those who had known about Roger had been in awe at the fine gentleman he had turned out to be. He made a big name for himself in the investment market. In addition, he had taken to going to church again; this time to receive God's blessings and to hear His word. Whenever he returned to the island, he asked to serve at the altar. The parish priest had been so impressed with the turn around that Roger had made, he always promised him a place at God's altar whenever he came home. As fate would have it, Roger had been in island that weekend. His eyes now took in the whole of Tricia from head to foot. Nothing had changed except that her curves were now fuller than before.

"I am coping" came the uncertain reply. Tricia followed up with a bright smile. It was the one she had practised too many times. It hid the suffering she experienced in her life. She hadn't wanted to tell anyone of her sins. Roger saw a distant pain in her eyes. He had known Tricia well. He was always the first to know when something just wasn't quite right. Because of his love for her, he had been attuned to her every expression. 'Lovesick' was the name his mother often called him. Tricia's eyes glanced down from his gaze now. She didn't want him to see through her lies.

Roger had seen her a few times while overseas. He always managed to stay out of sight for fear of spooking her. He still wasn't sure if she would want to speak to him. He would watch as she made her way to the front of the church to take up her rightful seat in the front pew as the wife of the invited Bishop. The churches that she visited were nothing like the ones back home. Most of them were at least five times the size of the largest church in Calvary or even Grenada. It wasn't that difficult to hide amongst the rest of the congregation, especially when she didn't expect to see him. Today was different. He wouldn't have been able to hide at the altar. As much as the women bombarded him while he was in Canada where he now lived, Roger had not been interested. He chalked it up to having more than his just share already. He was in a place in his life where he wanted a wife. When he had seen Tricia at the mission service in Las Vegas, he had been in awe all over again. She wore a cream coloured Michael Kors outfit that complimented her figure nicely. Her accessories had been navy blue in colour. Her bag matched the 5" heels that she wore. Her hair was pinned up in a tight bun and she wore a broad rimmed blue hat to accompany the bag and shoes. From where he sat her makeup had been somewhat flawless. She was stunning.

"I saw you the other day you know." Roger's voice was soft. She still brought out the little boy in him. He bowed his head after he made the comment.

Tricia was about to ask him where he had seen her when her husband interjected.

"Sweetheart, where have you been? I have been looking all over for you!" Elias too had skeletons in his closet. He was a jealous man. He prayed night and day asking God to forgive him and give him the strength to overcome this evil. It had become prominent after the night Tricia had thrown herself at him. He had secretly wondered if she wasn't satisfied with their love making. Since then, she had not approached him.

This had been unusual. Elias always had to be the one to get anything started, and even then, he wondered if she even enjoyed him. Once he was finished, Tricia would usually get up, take a bath, and go to sleep without a word. He was grateful she didn't try to attack him again, but his mind couldn't erase the fact that his wife had asked for more and he rejected her. Was she now getting sex elsewhere? Elias didn't want to think about it, but when he saw his wife talking to the likes of Roger Duncan he had been uneasy. It was several years since he last saw the man. He was surprised to see him serving at the altar when he visited today. While he knew it was not his place to judge, Roger had stolen one of Elias' girlfriends before. She was his first girlfriend, and though they had never so much as kissed, he had felt hurt when he found out Roger had gotten his hands on her. They had been merely 17 years old when Elias started courting Emily. He thought she would have been the one. Like Tricia, Emily was raised in a Christian family. Tricia had heard about the girl while she and Elias had been courting, but she couldn't say that she knew the quiet lass. Apparently the young people of the church had decided to go to the movies together. Elias had an exam the next day and opted to stay home. He dropped Emily off at the cinema to meet the group but Emily had gone alone. She had told Elias she would get a ride home with someone else so he need not bother himself from his studies. Sure enough, Roger offered her a ride when he realized that Elias wouldn't be coming back. Emily readily accepted as the person she had originally planned to hop a ride with had decided not to come after all. She lived far from the rest of the group; some 2 hours away. It wasn't too far for Roger though. He mentioned he was going to be in that area anyway so he had had no problem with giving Emily a ride that night. The movie finished after midnight. As luck would have it, Emily too had the cravings that every teen aged girl experiences. It hadn't been too hard for smooth talking Roger to get in her ear and between her legs. What happened next would have been any body's guess had it not been for the pictures. Many speculated that one of Roger's jealous women followed them and snapped pictures of them both with a special camera. They never saw a flash. Several times along the way Roger stopped and worked Emily over good. She had been a virgin. Her womanhood was tight and just right. Emily had been so much into it that she didn't flinch when Roger told her he was going to fuck her in the ass. She had orgasm after orgasm as Roger rammed into her hard, over and over again. They never realized they were being followed. In the dead of the night a camera was snapping away through his windshield. Each time they stopped the person got fresh pics of the two lovers. They had even been able to get a short video of the two as the windows of his truck had been partially rolled down. In short order, the pictures were up on the internet on a made up Facebook page. Cybercrime was still new to the Caribbean region so the police had been lost as to where to begin investigations. The person had gone as far as to steal one of Emily's innocent pictures from her real profile and named the new profile "Emily-The Baddest Bitch". By the time Emily got wind of the page, the entire of Calvary and Grenada had seen the pictures and the video. She could have died. The pictures showed her in all her naked glory at the mercy of Roger Duncan. The clarity and precision had almost been as if the person had been there in the truck with them and they were posing for a photo shoot. There were pics of her sucking his thick dick. Some showed him biting and licking her nipples. Yet others showed her orgasm as he fucked her hard in her wet pussy. The photographer had even succeeded in capturing a moment when he entered her and her juices started to squirt. It was an epic page. But the real prize had been the video. There was a short 2 minute clip of Roger smashing her ass. Emily had been heard on the clip pleading with Roger for anal sex. He had been whispering something but it hadn't been audible. But Emily was loud. You couldn't mistake her saying "Fuck me in the ass Roger! Put it in my ass!"

At one point Roger could be heard saying "your little choir boy could never fuck you like I can." Emily had vocally agreed while rocking her little ass back onto Roger for deeper penetration.

Anal sex was still somewhat taboo in the small islands. So to watch a quiet girl like Emily begging for this was more than the citizens could bear. The media had a field day with the information. Titles such as "Young Christian Whore", "Is This What They Teach in Sunday School" and "Sex- Ed for the Young Christian" soon flooded the newspapers. Her father had an instant heart attack. Her mother immediately packed her up and sent her by family that lived in England. She also sent a request to Facebook who immediately had the page shut down. Unfortunately, many of the young people had already downloaded the pictures and the video so it really didn't matter. Once Emily's father had been discharged from the hospital, the family packed up and moved without so much as a goodbye to their neighbours.

Elias barely lived through the ordeal. He first heard about it from a friend as he didn't have a Facebook page himself. Then he confronted Emily about what had happened that night. Not realizing that there were pictures of her doing the dirty, Emily had denied it profusely. It was only after Elias showed her a few pictures that she broke down in tears. Elias had been torn. He couldn't imagine such a sweet girl behaving in that manner. What had gotten into Emily was anyone's guess. On top of that he had been the joke of the town for the next few years. That was until he captured the heart of Tricia. She had heard about the episode and had been a comfort to Elias during that time. Little did she know he was secretly falling in love with her. No one ever spoke of Emily again. It was as if she disappeared into thin air. Of course Roger came out unscathed from that event. Actually, it made him even more wanted by the women in the country. He would receive many hushed requests, all of which he fulfilled with pleasure. Elias had never forgiven Emily or Roger. It was the one thing he fought with still as a Christian. He had already lost one woman to Roger Duncan. He would be damned if he lost his wife as well. And now, knowing that Tricia had some of the same erotic tendencies, he had become even more guarded.

Chapter 7

Roger excused himself and hastily retreated into the busy church yard where the other members of the congregation stood greeting each other. It was the usual Sunday morning picture. Persons who stood around were conversing about what had happened during the past week and filling each other in on their respective lives. Tricia's face fell as she watched Roger disappear into the crowd. She turned now to her husband quite annoyed.

"Now why did you go and run him off like that?" Tricia was upset. Of late she had been slightly intolerant of her husband's doings and he took notice.

"Why are you always so irritated all of a sudden Tricia? What is bothering you?"

Tricia sighed. She was not in the mood to thrash things out with her husband and she definitely wasn't about to air her dirty laundry in the church yard.

"I am ready to go home'" came the soft but firm reply.

Elias nodded. He quickly retrieved the couple's hired vehicle from its location in the rear of the church; a special area designated for priests. On returning, Tricia quietly got into the SUV and carefully closed the door. Elias continued out of the church gates, waving intermittently to the few remaining congregants.

"Nice service wasn't it?" It was all they talked about recently. Church, church and more church was the daily topic. Not that Tricia had a problem with talking about the Lord, but she was quite bored by the monotony of it all. Other things had been going on in life. There was politics that was now the talk of the town as elections were a mere 3 months away. Tricia enjoyed attending political meetings to hear what the different parties had to offer. Elias on the other hand feared being viewed as a member of a particular party and therefore stayed away. He had no clue what was going on in the political arena as he often said this country belongs to God and Him only shall he serve. It was his excuse not to get caught up in all the fiery conversations that ensued amongst the villagers. Tricia therefore was restricted to having these conversations with her friend Mrs. Bovell.

"It was lovely," she replied. She hadn't lied. She had enjoyed the service. The singing was lively and Tricia had sung her heart out. It was the only way she knew how to get close to the Lord.

The vehicle was quiet again. "So what did Roger want?"

Tricia rolled her eyes. It seemed as if every man that she spoke to lately was a problem for her husband. She really wasn't in the mood for his jealousy; especially since he hadn't exactly been doing much to keep her faithful!

Tricia blamed Elias for her infidelity. Why couldn't he just be the man she needed him to be? She had done everything right by him. She was a good wife. All she had wanted in return was a grateful husband. One who catered to her sexual needs. One who took interest in delighting her and making her crave him more. All Elias did was grunt and pant and sleep. She was sorely disappointed in their love making. Recently she took to making excuses whenever he approached her. She didn't find his lack of intimacy funny at all. Just because he was a man of God didn't mean he had to be boring for crying out loud.

"He didn't want anything. He just came by to say hello. And just as you butt in he was telling me he had seen me recently but I never got to finding out where." Tricia spoke in clipped tones. Elias knew that tone oh too well. It was one that had now become a norm in his home. He was now walking on eggshells around his wife. He couldn't understand exactly what was ticking her off all the time, and when he enquired, she would close right up even though he tried everything within his power to get her to open up to him.

The rest of the ride home had been quiet. Tricia disembarked the vehicle and hurriedly made her way into the house to finish preparing lunch. She had already gotten the ingredients prepped for her favourite dish oil down. Cooking was another one of Tricia's to- do things. She set her big pot out and brought out the ground provisions which she had peeled the night before. Her salted beef had already been prepped so she just dumped the remainder of the ingredients, together with the coconut milk in the pot and let it simmer. It kept her mind at ease as she moved effortlessly around her Victorian styled kitchen. It had cost her a pretty penny to purchase just the right appliances. The main part of the kitchen boasted of a large prep table in the middle where all the work was done. There was a fireplace in the centre of the far wall and a coal burning stove was also available for occasional use when she was in the mood. A large mahogany pie safe was located close to the pantry. It was where Tricia stored her breads and cakes that she loved to bake with her own hands. You would seldom find processed foods in Tricia's kitchen. She made her own cassava flour, baked her own breads, even her jams and cheeses were all made from scratch. She tried to preserve the natural state of foods where possible. In the main kitchen one could find a modern refrigerator, stove and microwave. The butler's pantry was located in a small attachment to the kitchen. Here, Tricia stored most of the raw materials for her dishes in the larder close by. The pantry was where the silverware and glassware were stored and polished. Table linens were also stored in this area. Tricia did the washing up in the scullery. Vegetables were washed in this area away from the main kitchen and brought in ready for preparation.

While Tricia was in the kitchen, Elias quietly retreated to his study to respond to some email. He seldom interfered when Tricia was in her zone. She cooked up a storm daily; so much so that there was seldom a need to purchase food to bring home. If you wanted to insult Tricia, buy food from somewhere else and you would feel her wrath. Elias had to hide and eat fast food whenever he had a craving. Not that Tricia couldn't cook; on the contrary. There were just times he felt to eat a little grease and salt. Elias' mind now drifted to his wife. She was indeed a wonderful woman. A man couldn't have asked for much more to be quite honest. She cooked for him daily. Many times in the pulpit he would joke and say that if Tricia ever fell ill or worst yet died, his own demise would soon follow. He always praised the work of his wife whenever he could. He was indeed grateful to have her in his life. Tricia had sacrificed much for him and his ministry. A qualified accountant by profession, Tricia had opted to give up her job and help Elias with his work.

"Well that is what any good wife would do no?" She had remarked. Elias had been humbled by the offer. He hadn't asked it of her but she had sought to make life for them much easier. Her work called for long hours as an auditor. And while Tricia had been paid extremely well at her level, she never once uttered a word of disappointment having given it all up. Ultimately, her dedication had been to her God and her husband. After Elias became Bishop of Calvary Isle, the demand for his attendance increased across the region. He had also been expected to travel the world and minister to those who called on him. Tricia had seen the increase in work her husband had to undertake. She ensured he got a full breakfast on mornings after their hour plus exercise session. She would prepare tasty yet healthy meals and snacks for him throughout the day. Dinner was always special to Elias. It was the only time Tricia permitted a "not as healthy" dessert. She always found some treat for Elias, but knowing his wife, he was always certain it was the healthier version to whatever recipe she had used. He loved her for loving him. Most Anglican priests proudly paraded their growing mid sections but Elias was chiselled thanks to his wife. It was not an easy task given all the events they were expected to participate in. And parishioners always tried to outdo each other with who could bring the best dish for their beloved Bishop. Tricia had been strict with Elias and his diet.

"You will take one forkful and one only" she would say. "That way, when they ask you how it tasted, you wouldn't have to lie". Many dishes Elias had longed to devour, but he knew Tricia was right. She always was. He couldn't afford to let himself go. As such, there was a thriving "Feed the Poor" programme in the community. Tricia had encouraged the young boys on the block to get up and make themselves useful by taking portions of food out to needy people every day. She would cut up whatever food was brought for Elias and place it in disposable containers which were delivered to those who needed it most; the receptors of which were always very grateful.

"These people seem not to realize that you have a wife" she would say daily. Most days at least 5 dishes would arrive by noon. Some even brought homemade juices for the Bishop. Tricia was always polite and exuberant when receiving the goodies. Most times her husband would be off doing God's work so he was hardly ever there to receive his gifts. Every week, she would remind him who he needed to call to show gratitude. This usually took up most of his Saturday mornings as he entertained the women, and even men, in a bit of conversation. Words such as lovely, delicious, and simply awesome became a regular part of his vocabulary. Many would ask how he managed to keep so trim and he would just laugh and say "my wife keeps my health in check". It definitely wasn't a lie.

Elias could smell the coconut milk permeating the walls of the house. Tricia didn't cook oil down too often, so when she did, he always ensured he got a hefty serving. It was a heavy food; one that sent you straight to sleep after consumption. A light wave of depression passed over Elias now. Not only was his wife a selfless woman and a great cook, she effortlessly took care of him and their home. Elias cannot tell anyone how to turn on his iron. Laundry was done very often in their home. While one load was in the dryer, another was in the washer and yet another was being ironed. This was a constant until every dirty piece of cloth was washed and ironed. Even their tablecloths and curtains were ironed. Not a wrinkle could be seen. And Tricia did this all herself. As for the cleaning, she always admitted she never liked the chemicals but she found a natural alternative and would give the house a good work over. Living so close to the road caused dust to settle in the house daily. It irritated Tricia to the point of obsession. When she wasn't cooking, she was cleaning, or polishing. The Parochial Church Council had offered on several occasions to get them a cleaner, but Tricia hated the idea of anyone in her home. "I need my privacy" she would say. It was bad enough that when anyone turned up unannounced to speak to her husband and sometimes even herself, she had to accept that and get on with God's work. She entertained many a broken woman in her home in between polishing the floors or rearranging the pantry. She was a sight to behold, balancing tears and sweat at the same time. For this Elias was grateful. He didn't know what he would do without Tricia. He would give her everything in the world if he could, but somehow he always felt as if he fell short; his mind now drifting to their love life. Tricia had made a request of him a few months ago; one he would never forget. His wife had seemed vulnerable yet in control. He must admit he was scared out of his wits until he was almost in tears. Sex wasn't something his folks spoke about. There are even still a few people who thought that he might be homosexual because he wanted to be a priest. This definitely had not been the case. Around age twelve, some of his older cousins had locked him in a room with pornography blaring from the media station. The moans and groans drove Elias to cower in a corner. He had squeezed his eyes shut to avoid seeing what was on the screen and he covered his ears to try to shut out the noise. It was summer and the boys had all been out of school on vacation. They always teased Elias saying he was strange and he needed to break out of it. This was their way of trying to bring him out of his shell. While Elias had been locked away, they ran two blocks down for Denise Prat. Elias had a soft spot for Denise and they knew it. They figured that all that porn would have aroused Elias beyond repair and they had planned to embarrass him in front of Denise. They were well shocked to open the door, and instead of seeing Elias with a stiffy from all the action, he was curled up in a corner praying. At that point Denise had gone in and "saved" Elias from the traumatic situation. She never spoke to his cousins again for what they had done to him. But then, Denise and her family moved to Greece as her father's job was relocated there and Elias never saw her again. Elias had not been one for porn or the perverted behaviour, and that being his first experience with it, never allowed him to open his mind to such things, even within the marriage setting.

He could hear Tricia humming now. She usually did once she was happy. He breathed a sigh of relief. At least she was somewhat pacified for the time being. All he had to do was ensure she stayed that way.

CHAPTER 8

Tricia glided around the kitchen. She was enjoying her time there. Cooking always made her happy; though she didn't eat half of what she cooked. She was a small eater. Always being fearful of catching some non-communicable disease that she wouldn't be able to manage, Tricia ensured she and her husband ate well. Her cooking almost always went to someone who needed the food much more than she did. But she loved to cook. That was for certain. She hummed as she worked. It always calmed her soul. Lately she had needed this calming as her sins had been catching up with her. On the drive home, all she could think about was Roger's last statement. Where on earth could he have seen her? She recounted her steps the last few months. She had been to Germany for a conference, Hong Kong for a wedding ceremony and to Detroit to complete a training course the church had asked her to do. She hadn't been anywhere near Canada so she wasn't sure exactly where Roger had seen her. This bothered her somewhat. With the type of activities she often got up to while on these trips, she couldn't afford for anyone to pick her up. She had tried to be so discrete. Well, actually, she hid in plain sight. Everything occurred at the hotel she was staying at. She couldn't afford to be seen traipsing about in a strange country. It was also for her safety. Her husband would know where she was and the church knew where she was. That being the case, it was safer for her to be at the hotel than to go out and risk being kidnapped or something worst. All her activities occurred there. There had been no dinners or clubbing, just strictly visits. She always asked her boy toys to come dressed decently. The hotel was always informed that she would be expecting visitors at all hours because of her profile. It came then as no surprise when men and women found their way to see the Bishop's wife before she left the country.

Absentmindedly, she had moved to a small drawer in her mahogany desk. It was a small desk where she often times sat to rest her feet while she was in the kitchen. Underneath the desk was a small compartment that could hardly be seen by the naked eye. The desk itself was an antique. Designed some hundred years ago, Tricia had had the piece sanded and refurbished to its original glory. It was on its return that the gentleman had shown her the secret compartment. She never had reason to hide anything from her husband, but the letter she received a few weeks ago was more than enough reason to do so now. It had outlined her activities a cold winter night. It was almost as if the person had been in the room with her and Marcus. After reading the letter that first time, Tricia had contacted Marcus and had threatened to sue for breach of contract. How dare he go back on his word? She had told him she would shut down his business by spreading the word that he could not be trusted. Quietly, Marcus took in everything that Tricia spat at him. When she was finished he simply replied, "It wasn't me, but you definitely have a problem on your hands."

With that, Marcus ended the call leaving Tricia feeling bewildered. She hadn't really believed it was him. These are the very principles these businesses thrived on; confidentiality was key. But who could have seen her and how did they know such intimate detail? The letter read:

"I didn't know you liked it so rough. And your hair, your beautiful hair...how could you let him treat you that way?"

Marcus had grabbed a fistful of Tricia's curls as he rammed her from the back. Tricia remembered that session well. It was the first time she had been totally submissive, and she had loved it. Marcus had grabbed her neck in a passionate rage and had kissed her breathless. He licked and bit his way all over her body causing her pain and pleasure at the same time. Tricia had begged him for more. Marcus all but brutalized Tricia. At one point she just couldn't shut up. She was hyped out and on the edge with excitement.

"Hush your filthy mouth" came the demand. "This is my show doll" Marcus was teasing her. He had taken her close to her peak and dead stopped. His tongue had done some considerable damage to her clitoris.

When he entered her hotel room that night, Marcus promised her a fucking of a lifetime.

"It's different when you actually find your client beautiful" he swooned. She was definitely a beauty, but he had had a job to do. When Tricia contacted his business, she indicated she was looking for a man to make her beg; one that could make her cum uncontrollably and squirt even. Marcus was known for this. He contacted her the same time and indicated she was going to have a hell of a ride when he got his hands on her. Those words alone had thrilled Tricia. She had been eager to reach her destination to experience what Marcus had to offer. As he stripped down to his spandex boxer shorts, Tricia could see his cock printing through the thin material in splendour. Eagerly she rushed to grab it. On her way to her knees, Marcus grabbed her under her chin.

"No no no... I am the boss in here tonight" he had said. With that, he threw her onto the bed and began to slowly tease her. Tricia swore his tongue had belonged to an ox. It was thick and beefy. Its fullness ran its course all over her body. At one point he flipped her over and began to stick his teeth into her ass. This forced Tricia to arch her back; her body craving more. Marcus could feel the excitement mounting in her. Hooking his well-defined arm under her midsection, Marcus easily dragged her off the bed to a standing position. He bent her in half and bound her ankles and wrist together using bondage tape; she was in a perfect inverted letter "V". Tricia was about to protest. She had never been bound before and while it was exciting, many thoughts crossed her mind. Suppose he left her in that state? Suppose he wouldn't stop when she asked him to? Before she had realized what was going on, both her hands had been restrained and her pussy was exposed for him to take advantage of. And that he did. Marcus constantly told her how beautiful she was. That he wished he had a woman like her in his bed every night.

"Your husband doesn't know what to do with you does he?" He asked this as he allowed his hands to explore her body. He kissed the inside of her thighs gently causing her to shudder.

"You are so fucking beautiful Tricia." She moaned. His words were driving her insane. His hands moved methodically over her body, as if her were an artist molding a piece of clay. Between the squeezing and the gentle licking, Tricia could feel herself nearing explosion. With both legs spread wide and her head hanging close to the ground, Tricia found herself trying to gyrate to get him to taste her.

"Tell me what you want baby. I want to please you tonight." Her juices started to spring. His voice was soft yet firm. The huskiness caused a pool to form between her legs. Marcus moved his face closer to her vagina. He could see the shine oozing out from his prize. But he wasn't ready as yet. He was going to take his time with this one. In her email, she had told him she had never been in submissive positions before. The excitement bubbled in Marcus now. He gently kissed all around her vagina; avoiding the core of her womanhood. He felt her start to wine; willing him to stick his tongue in. As much as he wanted to taste her, he refrained. He took two fingers and gently opened her lips. God, she was wet.

"You ready for some good loving baby?"

"Yes….please…yes" she was almost in tears now. His kisses were driving her insane. Tricia felt a draft. She could see Marcus had shifted his position, and leaned for something in his bag. She couldn't see what it was. Soon, he was standing behind her. She felt a few drops of some liquid hit one half of her ass, and then Marcus grabbed her again. It was massage oil. On his knees now, he worked his hands and sniffed her. Tricia was going crazy.

"Taste me Marcus!" Marcus let his tongue slide just over her closed lips. Her clit had been peeking so much that it protruded from the lips that housed it. Tricia moaned. Marcus grabbed both lips and began to massage them. They were still closed, but the massage applied pressure in all the right places. He picked up the pace and she squirmed uncontrollably. She wanted to feel either his fingers or his tongue inside of her, but Marcus had other things in mind. Her ass was gleaming from the oils he had placed on it. His hot breathe touched her skin at differing points pushing Tricia closer to her destination. When Marcus realized she was about to bust, he slid one finger in her ass. This caused Tricia to jerk. She had never been fingered in her ass before. That shit felt good. By the fifth stroke her juices squirted straight into his waiting mouth; but Marcus didn't stop there. He continued to ram his thick finger in her butt while her body convulsed. His tongue now snaked its way out of his mouth and dived deep into her womanhood. The pressure coming from both ends was more than Tricia could bear. Her voice escalated as she felt her body shake again. "Holy shit Marcus" she had cried. Her captor didn't stop. He worked her even deeper with his tongue. Her juices now covered his face. He took her clit in his mouth and began a gentle sucking. With his free hand, Tricia felt another thick finger make its way deep inside her vagina. This is what heaven must feel like. Without so much as another thought, Tricia's body shook a third time. Back to back orgasms took over her body as Marcus skilfully teased her over and over again. Soon, he stopped and let her body ease back down from the pleasure. That had gone better than he had expected. Now fully hyped, Marcus released Tricia from her bonds. Her body collapsed onto the floor as her legs gave way. Dragging her to her feet, Marcus kissed her passionately. Between her legs was wet and messy, just how Marcus liked it.

"I promised you this would be a fucking of a lifetime, and that it will be! Prepare to be fucked out of your mind Tricia." Marcus had whispered in the depth of her neck. Her hard nipples pressed against his chest. He could feel them aroused through the thick curls that covered him. Instinctively, he reached up and plucked one. Her body was driving him over the edge. She responded to his every motion and he loved it.

She glowed. If that teaser was anything to go by, Marcus would be by far the best lover she had had to date. Marcus stood behind her now, sniffing her hair. With one swift shove, she was face down on the bed. Not knowing what to expect, Tricia rolled over with a look of uncertainty on her face.

"Did I tell you to turn over?" Marcus' jawline tightened. Tricia couldn't tell if he was angry or joking. She opened her mouth to reply. Before she could utter a word, a strong stinging slap swung her face to one side. "Did I tell you to speak?" Fear clouded Tricia now. She hastily tried to pry herself from between Marcus' legs. Feeling her sudden movement, Marcus climbed further up her body, straddling her across her chest.

"You asked for this dick, and you're going take it" came his whisper. "You are mine tonight Tricia. I will fuck you every which way I know how."

With that, he tugged the waist of his boxer and the entire thing flew off as the Velcro unhinged itself. Marcus was over her breasts now and his large penis hung heavy over her lips. Helping her raise her head slightly, Marcus rubbed the tip of his dick on her mouth. She had some beautiful lips.

"You know how to suck a dick miss?" Tricia nodded. She had honestly never sucked anything that big but she wasn't in a position to say no. Slowly she opened her mouth to receive him. Knowing the girth of his penis, Marcus moved slowly. He looked down and watched Tricia enjoy pleasing him. That bitch had skill. She twirled her tongue around the tip and then sucked gently on his head. Marcus moaned. He shifted his body just a little so she could take control. Tricia brought up her hands and grabbed the shaft of his penis. It was hot to touch. Unable to control himself, Marcus began to move his waist to the rhythm of her tongue. He pulled back on several occasions not wanting to cum prematurely; feeling his desire mount up. Tricia now shifted positions. Without him realizing it, Marcus had somehow ended up on his back. Tricia didn't miss a beat. She lowered her mouth onto him and made him swear. His toes began to curl and Tricia picked up the pace. Grabbing her hair, Marcus aided Tricia in her endeavour. She began to deep throat his cock, taking in that entire bad boy.

"My God Tricia," Marcus exclaimed. She sucked like a porn star. Moments later, Marcus felt himself shifting into another gear. Tricia's mouth was opened wide. Without further words between them, Marcus exploded down Tricia's throat. Tricia gagged. She had never tasted sperm before. In trying to catch her breath from all that sucking, a huge gulp went down her throat as Marcus further drained himself in her mouth. There has been nothing left to do but swallow.

Marcus was fiery now. This was supposed to be his parade. She had no right pleasuring him. This isn't what she had paid for. Stretching his body horizontally over hers, Marcus stuck his tongue into her ear. "Time for the real ride precious." Tricia wrapped her legs around his waist intuitively, but Marcus had other things in mind. Grabbing her by her throat, he dragged her back to her feet and bent her again at the waist. Her hands fell onto the bed this time and her ass was raised. 'WHACK' Tricia swore Marcus left his handprint in her flesh.

"A little rough there love" she pined. Rough? Wasn't that what she had asked for? 'WHACK' the other ass cheek received just as much love. Her firm bottom jumped as Marcus abused it. This was exciting Tricia again. She could hear Marcus pulling on his condom. In this job one could never be too safe. One of the prerequisites for this service was to have a recent HIV test result to present; as recent as the previous week to the meeting. You are also required to sign a form indicating that to the best of your knowledge you are free from all STDs and are therefore not passing anything on to the service provider. Tricia had always had her tests done. She took this part very seriously because you never knew when a condom could burst. That and her birth control were always in her bag. She also took time to scrutinize the paperwork of the man coming to her as well. She couldn't afford to take home anything to her husband after all. Marcus had been clean, but he wanted to enjoy torturing Tricia for a bit before he took the dive. On hearing her protest to the slaps, Marcus held her in what he called the 'choke and stroke' hold. From his position behind her, he firmly grabbed her by the neck. Before Tricia could enquire as to what was happening, Marcus entered her from behind. A moan escaped from Tricia as Marcus began to pump in this position. Still holding her neck, Tricia found herself with minimal movement room. Marcus curved his pelvis under and that aided him in hitting just the right spot. She felt him deep in her core. The intensity grew as Marcus swiftly moved in and out of her while intermittently squeezing her vocal cords. With her head arched back, Marcus gently released her neck and now grabbed a fistful of hair; his strokes still firm and strong. Tricia spread her knees to accept him a bit deeper. She was enjoying this. Her moans escalated to higher strengths. His strokes were supplemented with "is this how you like it" and "tell me what you want".

"I want it! I want it Marcus! Fuck me dirty!" Tricia was begging for the dick. She was soon nearing her end again. Marcus could feel her walls tightening up around him. He quickly pulled out after she had had her fill. He wasn't ready to cum himself. Flipping her onto her back, Marcus pulled her ass over the edge of the bed, pressed her knees as close to her shoulders as she could manage and slid deep in her. Tricia's pelvis was now curved upwards and Marcus was pounding deep inside her belly. It was the first love making that made Tricia curse like a pirate. Marcus' dick was nothing to play with. He went deeper and deeper as he felt her nails dig into the skin on his back. As he felt himself nearing combustion, he slid out of the condom so he could feel her. When he re-entered there was nothing that could stop what happened next. Marcus went weak; his strokes hastening now as he could hardly bear the sensation. God almighty she was wet. He pounded; Tricia held on tight. Soon she felt her volcano erupt between her legs. Marcus felt it too. He soon lost control. In all his years in the business, none had ever done the damage that Tricia had done in such a short space of time.

That had been one hell of a night. Tricia got the hours she had paid for and much more. She was one client Marcus did not want leave.

CHAPTER 9

Tricia shook herself out of the trance. She smelt the pot beginning to burn as it simmered on low heat. She had gotten so caught up in the memory that she forgot about the stove. Quickly, she replaced the letter in its hiding place and she rushed to check on her dish. Stirring with a big spoon, Tricia was content that the food was still very much palatable. Soon, Elias' head peeked around the corner.

"All is well in here?" he asked. He had begun to smell the burning himself and was pretty surprised. Something must have been wrong. Tricia never burnt a thing in her life except a candle.

"All is well love" Tricia replied. "Just a bit of underestimation on the timing that is all. Lunch is ready Hun." With that, Tricia turned off the burner and moved to set the table. She placed the customary wine glasses and water goblets in their places. Wine and water were a staple with every meal. They both enjoyed a nice glass of wine. Their wine cooler was never empty. She then dished out the soupy oil down into some medium sized dishes and placed them in their rightful positions on the marble top dining table. Elias was eager for his meal. Not only was he hungry, but Tricia was a darn good cook. He sat at his usual place at the head of the table. Looking through a massive window straight ahead, Elias could see the Greasleys making their way up the unpaved path. The two year old barely able to keep up with his older brothers and sisters could be seen tottering on behind the bunch. Mrs. Greasley could be heard cautioning the group even though traffic hardly ever made its way through the gap. It was a cosy and friendly neighbourhood. Everyone looked out for each other. In her usual spot, Mrs. Greasley paused and looked in the direction of the window. As customary, she raised her hand

and waved to the Bishop and his wife. It was too far a distance to have a conversation, but she never failed to acknowledge her neighbours on her daily treks past their home. Tricia smiled warmly. She could set her clock by that wave. The Greasleys passed by the same time every Sunday afternoon.

Elias now refocused on his home. He was a lucky man. He owned three houses and he owed it all to his beautiful wife. Were it left up to him, they would be moving from home to home in the church system. There was one in Calvary Isle which Tricia had suggested they invest in. She had insisted they build their own place back on her homeland. They rented it out to the high end market. It was Tricia's baby. She loved real estate. If she could spend all of her money in buying and refurbishing houses she would. It had not been enough that they had redone her parents' home. But Elias had known it was a good idea. When it came to money, Tricia knew how to cut and contrive and best of all, invest. When she was working as the Regional Chief Financial Officer for Flour Creations Inc., Tricia saved as much as she could to build that house. It had to be everything short of perfect for the clientele she had envisioned it for. She had purchased an acre of land up on a hill overlooking the Caribbean Sea. The land had been a hard sell, but Tricia had a vision for the property. The owner had been more than pleased to get it off his hands.

"What are you going to do with this uneven land?" he asked Tricia. She promised him that when she was finished he wouldn't even have recognised it. She got to researching on the best use of the land. She had a good idea what she wanted, but she needed to make sure it made structural sense. The house was actually built into the side of the hill. Nothing could be built in front of it to dampen the view. The three story mansion was adorned with marble tiles in every room and granite countertops. The furniture had been hand crafted mahogany with quality upholstery. Tricia had gone as far as outfitting each room with their respective pieces of furniture. Anyone could walk in and start to live without as much as a visit to a store short of purchasing food. Each of the smaller bedrooms held its own Queen Sized bed. There were matching chest of drawers, fireplaces, side tables and dressers as well. Each bedroom had its own walk in closet. Though much smaller than the master suite, the bedrooms were a picture of luxury and comfort. There had been wall to wall carpeting with a thick furry covering. It was like walking on air. The master suite itself was a sight to behold. Tricia had gone mad decorating this space. The bathroom was massive. A private hot tub was off to one corner, surrounded by teak wood. The shower was littered with exquisite mosaic tiles. The porcelain pieces glistened and the cabinetry was well polished. The fixtures and fittings too had been carefully chosen. A British aura permeated each room. The master bedroom had its own sitting area. There was a small two-seater glass top dining set and a full living room suite off to one side; close to the fireplace. Double French doors lead to a massive patio which overlooked the ocean. To the short left, one could see an Olympic sized pool and an attached hot tub. The garden was delicate yet superb. The flora boasted of several local and international trees and plants which adorned a well-manicured lawn. The grass alone had cost a pretty penny. Tricia had insisted on having a pond with real fish. There was a small waterfall cascading off a small rocky cliff created by the resident gardener. It truly was beautiful scenery. Elias often wondered how the persons that rented the place could even leave to go to work on mornings. He figured he could spend all day in the garden alone as it was so peaceful. When Tricia was done with the place, only one ad made it into the local newspapers before several organizations were calling to rent the house for their executives. There was so much competition, that they started to try to outbid each other. Being the business person that she is, Tricia rented to the highest bidder with the longest contract terms. They received three times what they were originally planning to rent the place for. With a guaranteed contract for ten years, Tricia had begun paying off the mortgage at a much faster rate than expected. Soon, the house was paying for itself and they were on to another project. The house he was currently in had been his first home after moving out from his parents' place. When Tricia had first suggested they renovate the place he was hesitant. At that time he was a priest. He had grown attached to the place as it was and didn't want the congregation to think he was taking the church's money to create a place of luxury.

"You are aware I am an executive at one of the largest firms in Caribbean right?" Tricia had not been amused. Not that she had an issue living in a chattel house, but she didn't exactly go to school to stay one place all her life. She wanted to live and enjoy life and all that it had to offer. She believed in travelling and taking care of her body, mind and health. Tricia could be found often receiving spa treatments. She was a woman who took care of herself and the Anglicans know this. Not a hair is ever out of place. Her nails are always immaculately done and her clothing of very high quality. Elias knew that when Tricia had given up her high paying job to work with him as Bishop, she had given up a lot of worldly things. By that time however, Tricia had already rented their place in Calvary and had had enough collateral to renovate the current home that they were in. Because they spent so much time back and forth in Grenada, Tricia had figured it would make more sense to own a home there as well. In the early days they had tried to stay at hotels, but it proved too costly. As usual, Tricia was right. It was cheaper for them to pay a mortgage on a modest home than to stay in a hotel. While the Anglican Church always housed their priests, they had refused the home offered to them. Tricia had said that it could be used for another priest or for community activities. She made enough money that they did not have to burden the church's pockets with their upkeep. While she had taken this stance, she refused to lower her standards but always operated well within their means. This house was small compared to the mansion on the other island. Since this was where home would be on the main land, Tricia had ensured it was comfortable. The only thing she asked was that she have a big kitchen to operate in. Elias knew just how much she loved to cook so he had given his blessing. Besides the lunches that were sent to him daily, many meals were cooked in the kitchen for the homeless and needy. Tricia had purchased some industrial sized saucepans for this venture, and daily you could hear the pots banging as she moved about to feed the less fortunate.

The other home was also in Calvary. It was where they lived once they were in the island. It was a modest place. Many people didn't even know they had owned the first house; certainly not the congregations. It wasn't that they had anything to hide, but Caribbean people loved to talk, even if they didn't know what they were talking about. Tricia was a private person, and though many knew she had had an executive job, they could only hazard a guess at what her income had been like. Tricia had comfortably been able to apply for the two mortgages. The bank didn't even think twice about signing her up. Soon, after she had gotten the first house rented out with that long term contract, she was able to free up her money again as the house paid for itself. This second house though was in the heart of Calvary. It was close to the people that they served. Everyone knew and loved them in the community. Tricia always joked that they had unpaid security as the neighbours always watched out for them when they weren't on island. She always knew which of the boys had climbed the mango tree. Or who sat on their front wall. They never really minded, but felt a comfort in knowing that their home was safe when they were not there.

"How was lunch?" Tricia's words roused her husband from his daze. Making sure he was well fed was one of the things Tricia had dedicated herself to. She truly did love Elias. She would have sacrificed everything she had for him; and mostly she did too. Now that Tricia was no longer in the business world, her weekly treatments were now down to a minimum; necessity only. While she didn't allow herself to run to ruins of any sorts, she had opted now to do most of her grooming herself instead of paying someone to do it for her. Her weekends were filled with perming and curling her long mane. She had purchased all the things required to give herself regular pedicures and facials. She had even mastered the art of manicuring her fingers without help. She loved to look nice. It always boosted her spirits; though she always remained humble about her beauty.

"It was lovely my dear," Elias droned. He had asked for seconds during the course of the meal which Tricia gladly obliged. She never really packed the plates anyway. One of those healthy techniques she had instilled. That way, if seconds were had, one would not be over eating in any event. Elias was now heavy from the hearty meal. He got up from his seat and planted a firm kiss on Tricia's forehead. As she watched her husband walk from the room, water sprung to her eyes again as she remembered all the naughty things she had been getting herself up to. If Elias ever found out, he would be devastated.

CHAPTER 10

The wind hooked the peach curtains as it blew through the large windows of their comfy bedroom. Elias had retreated there after the lovely lunch Tricia had prepared for him. Fatigued and pleasantly filled, Elias stretched across the outdoor sofa which was sitting on their private patio. Here is where he planned most of his sermons. The flow of the wind fed his mind and took him to a place of peace and happiness. It was also the place where he pondered about his marriage. Recently, this had been his major concern. While he and Tricia never argued, he was beginning to feel a distance between them that he didn't like. Physically she was there; always by his side and always supporting him. Mentally, she provided him with strong connection as they planned each week together. From which meals would be served to the less fortunate, to what clothes he would be wearing even to which upcoming trips they would attend. Emotionally however, Elias felt like he was living with a stranger.

In the living room downstairs, Tricia sat deep in thought. She hadn't felt to sleep just yet as her mind was still reeling from the conversation she had with Roger that morning. She was at a total lost as to where he could have seen her. And worst yet, was he brazen enough to send her that letter? Tricia needed answers. The Roger she knew in times gone by was fairly immature, however, he never dared to step on her corns. She knew he had felt badly that he never got a chance to be with her, but his actions and reputation were nothing that Tricia wanted in her life. Nevertheless, she was sure he had matured now. He was no longer the horny teenager hopping from bed to bed; he was now a man who had to take full responsibility for his actions. During the course of the conversation, Roger mentioned that he was staying at the Hilton Hotel for a few days. The old house he used to live in was rented out, so whenever he was in island, he had to find somewhere to stay. This was never a problem for Roger as he liked to stay out of the limelight anyway. Caribbean people didn't forget anything. If you wanted a good biography, don't go to the person who lived the life, go to someone who knew them. You would be guaranteed to hear of things that the main character themselves didn't even know. He was certain no one forgot about his past, and being that he was trying to be a changed man, he felt the need to stay as far away from the negativity as he could.

Tricia picked up the telephone with the intention of calling the hotel. She needed to get to the bottom of this. If it was Roger that sent her that letter, she knew she would be furious on one hand, but relieved on the other for putting the final piece of the puzzle in place. After dialling the number, the phone rang. Butterflies began to flutter in the pit of her stomach. What would she ask him when he answered? Tricia hadn't thought that far. The voice on the other end jumped her out of her daze.

"Good Afternoon, thank you for calling Hilton Grenada, how may I direct your call?" A chirpy voice flowed through the phone enquiring on how it would be able to assist Tricia. She froze.

"Am…I think I have the wrong number" Quickly Tricia replaced the handset onto the cradle. She needed to think some more. She couldn't exactly call without first having a plan in place. Rocking back in the leather recliner, Tricia drifted further into thought. Nothing made sense at this point. If Roger had seen her, why would he have been concerned about how she had been treated during the sexual encounter? He probably would have been more concerned as to why he never got the chance to do the things that were done to her. It couldn't be Roger; it just couldn't have been him! Tricia's brows wrinkled. This letter had been causing her so much grief that her entire body ached at times. She knew it was the stress of not knowing. She had to find out. Taking a few minutes more, Tricia devised a plan of conversation. She would be frank yet evasive. Give as much information as she could without actually giving away the content of the letter; or worst yet her fear or worry. Supposed he tried to blackmail her? What would she do? She just couldn't afford for this news to get out. It would bring down her entire world as she knew it.

Having satisfied herself with how the conversation would go, Tricia boldly took up the handset again. This time, when the friendly receptionist asked to be of assistance, Tricia readily accepted.

"Can you kindly patch me through to Roger Duncan's room please?"

"Sure, kindly hold," came the soft reply. Mr. Killa's famous song "Rolly Polly" started to flow through the pipeline. Tricia jumped, but then recalled it was soon Carnival season again on the Spice Isle. Most hotels gave their local artistes air play as a way to give those visiting the island a taste of what the festival had to offer. While it generally wasn't Tricia's taste in music, she found herself rocking to the catchy rhythm. Soca was the essence of the Caribbean. Each island had produced their top performers. Once it had a good rhythm for people to move their waist and gyrate too, it was a hit in these islands. You would even find other countries supporting artistes from outside of their own shores. It was a massive business.

Soon, the music paused.

"I am sorry ma'am, there was no answer on his end, would you like me to try again or do you want to leave a message?" Disappointment crept across Tricia's face. She had hoped to talk to Roger today.

"Try one more time and if you still don't reach him I will leave a message." That was the most she could do. She figured Roger had probably gone to lunch with a friend after church.

"Sure ma'am, please hold the line again." The music restarted and Tricia's mind drifted once again. Every year there was always some form of controversy over the Carnival music that came out. The Christians usually raised a fuss about how "uncouth" the young people were. They would abuse the name of the artiste who made the "disgusting and distasteful" song. Tricia usually avoided these conversations as they made no sense to her. God gave each of us the free will to walk this earth and live as we see fit. While he would prefer that we live in his image, God is an all knowing and forgiving God. Why then do we find the need to cast judgement on those who behave differently to us when God asks us not to judge? As far as Tricia was concerned, she had her own taste in music and as such, she just listened to that instead of working herself up about the other genres that existed.

Again, there was a break in the music. "I am sorry ma'am but Mr. Duncan seems not to be in at this point. May I take your message?" Tricia sighed.

"Sure, tell him that Tricia Dessington called and would like him to give her a call please."

"Mrs. Dessington, as in the wife of the Bishop of Calvary?"

"Yes, that Mrs. Dessington." Tricia smiled. It was always funny how she seemed to have lost her identity after she married Elias. Shortly after he had been ordained they got married. She had then become 'the wife of Father Dessington'. Now, she was almost always known as 'the wife of the Bishop of Calvary'. Tricia often wondered if people even remembered her maiden name! Not that she was offended of course; on the contrary. It was the life that she had chosen when she walked down the aisle. After Tricia confirmed her mobile number with the receptionist, she settled the handset back into its resting place. All she could do for now was to wait for Roger to return her call.

CHAPTER 11

Roger stepped out of the bath tub a bit frustrated. He had heard when the phone rang the first time but he refused to move. He figured the caller would think he wasn't available and leave a message. Not many people knew where he was staying anyway so he thought it must be front desk calling him. When the phone rang the second time, Roger sighed heavily. He had just finished lunch and had opted to take a soak in the hotel's extra-large tub. As he was staying in one of their most luxurious suites, Roger wanted to enjoy as much of his stay as he possibly could. Clearly his caller had other things in mind. In his haste to exit the tub, Roger's wet foot slid on the towelled mat when it hit the floor at a funny angle. He was able to prevent any serious mishap, but not before he had slid far enough to hurt his groin.

"Good Lord!" he spat and he tried to regain his footing. Once balancing again on two feet, Roger slowly raised his body to the standing position and made sure everything was still in working order. Short of the sharp pain that generated between his leg, Roger was good. Soon, the phone rang off again. There was a short beep after indicating that a message had been left this toss. Good, Roger thought, at least now he would know who to call and tell off for almost splitting him in half! "The devil is always hardest at work when you are trying to walk the Godly path" he muttered. Taking his time now, Roger towelled his entire body to rid it of the droplets that had remained from his soak. He didn't want to walk on the tiles with a wet body in case he really did end up hurting himself. Once he was satisfied that he was dry enough, he proceeded to his bedroom to find out who his impatient caller was. Sitting butt naked on the edge of the bed, he dialled the four digit code that had been presented to him when he had checked in. This would retrieve the message for him.

"4:37 PM. From: Marian from the front desk" the machine started the process of retrieving the message for him. "Good Evening Roger, this is front desk calling to inform you that you received a call when you were unavailable. The caller was Mrs. Dessington, the wife of the Bishop of Calvary. Her number is..." At that point Roger had stopped listening. The mere sound of Tricia's name sent shivers down his spine. Tricia had called for him? What could she possibly want? He had been so caught up in his own thoughts that he missed the number.

"To listen to this message again, press one. To delete it, press 2. To be routed to our front desk department, press zero." Roger quickly pressed one and took note of the number on the stationery that Hilton had provided. He played the message two more times to ensure he had gotten the number absolutely correct. Why was he so easily flustered by this woman? She is married for crying out loud he reminded himself. Roger sat on the edge of his bed staring at the 7 digits before him. She must really want something important to be calling him, he thought. Maybe she was just being nice after her husband whisked her away today. She might just want to apologise. Roger thought that Elias had been very rude. Elias hadn't even acknowledged him, but just swooped down to "rescue" his wife no less. Roger smiled to himself. It wasn't like he and the man had been buddies growing up anyway. Roger still remembered the fiasco he had gotten himself into with Amy. He never found out who had been tailing them; and quite frankly he never cared. Elias was a punk. Just because he was a priest didn't mean he was God's gift to the world; especially to Tricia. Roger had seen a distant pain in her eyes when he had enquired about how she had been keeping. "I'm managing" she had said. Which happily married woman says that? Clearly something was going on and Roger wanted to get to the bottom of it. He had never spoken again to Elias after that situation so many years ago. Even as they served at the altar together that morning, there had been a slight tension between the two. Roger moved about his business as did Elias without their paths ever having to meet. He had seen the glare that Elias had given him when he first entered the altar that morning. He politely nodded and quickly moved to put the Chalice in its rightful place until it was time for communion. When Elias presented himself to the chatting pair after church, Roger could feel the territorial air surround them.

He had quickly retreated; not wanting to cause any problems for Tricia. Tricia...Roger stared at the paper again. He would return the call, but not yet. He would wait until later in the evening when he knew Elias would be at the Church Council meeting. It had been announced in the notices that morning and Roger was most sure Tricia would have been alone. Maybe the two of them could have dinner and catch up he thought. Dinner was innocent enough. Not that he was inviting her to his room or anything; even though that would have been the highlight of his trip. No. Roger would be respectful. Tricia had made her decision and he wasn't the one. It was a reality that haunted Roger all his life.

Roger struggled to focus now. There were a few things he needed to do. He decided to go out and run his errands and come back to finish up some work before he called Tricia. His world couldn't stop because of one phone call. Mrs. Alleyne, his late mother's good friend, had invited him over. Once his mother had passed, she had insisted that Roger keep in contact with her. She was his mother's best friend and her passing had been a massive hit to the old woman. Actually, Roger had thought that she too would have died. The day he left for Canada, he promised Mrs. Alleyne that he would check in on her every week, regardless of where he was. Roger had kept that promise for the past ten years, and now that he was in the island, he would give the old girl a visit. He found she was always full of objective wisdom and he could talk to her for hours about any problems that he had. And, like his mother, she always enquired as to when he would get married and provide her with grandbabies. Mrs. Alleyne never had children of her own but she had always treated Roger like a son. He appreciated this most days, especially when his mom had to work late. Roger could be found having dinner over at Mrs. Alleyne on those nights until his mother came home. Once he left school on evenings he was to walk straight to that house. As a former school teacher, Mrs. Alleyne would help Roger with his homework, provide him with a warm meal and ensured he got a bath and changed his clothes by the time his mother arrived. Since his mother worked shift, Roger spent half his evenings at home, and the other half by Mrs. Alleyne. In his teenage years the woman had openly wept about his escapades. Usually ranting about how his mother tried to raise him to be a gentleman, Mrs. Alleyne berated his newfound love for sex and his exploitations. She and his mother could be found on the phone every day trying to figure out "what to do with that young boy now". It wasn't that Roger had turned against the two women; he was just at a point in his life where he had needed to connect with his dad. No-one ever spoke of his father in front of him, but he had been teased about him at school. Many nights Roger would cower in his room when his mother thought he was asleep and cry. He couldn't understand why his father didn't want him; didn't love him. He was no different to many non-existent dads in the Caribbean. Probably one in every five men goes missing from their families and don't support their children. This was nothing strange to the islands and neither Calvary nor Grenada had been exempt from this parental disease. Not all children recover from the trauma of being fatherless however. Actually, most children carry the depression into their adult life and tend to either mimic the missing piece of the puzzle or shy away from the characteristics of the person that hurt them. Children really do have impressionable minds. Roger had fought feverishly for his dad's attention. The old man had approached him one day and Roger had been ecstatic. He was around eighteen years old at the time. While Roger had thought that he had finally gotten through to his dad, he had been sent into a further depression by what occurred next. Apparently one of the women that the older Duncan had been dealing with decided she had wanted a taste of the son. When she realised she couldn't make his father settle down and marry her, she used Roger to get back at his father. Soon after she finished sexing the life out of Roger, she contacted his dad and let him know his son was a better fuck than he ever was. At first the old man didn't believe her, but then she described the birthmark near his groin that looked like a rum bottle. Many days he and Roger's mother had joked that their son was destined to a life of rum drinking, so that, if nothing else, had stuck with the old man. That day when he approached his son, he had had nothing for him but a string of dirty words. The cussing left many in the streets in disgust. As old as Roger was at the time, he had cried. He was torn to the core by the things his father said to him. He hadn't known the woman was one that belonged to his dad; how could he? But his father was more interested in his ego than anything else. When he finished lambasting the young boy on the pavement, he pushed past him and had never spoken a word to him since then. This sent Roger further into his waywardness. Searching for love in all the wrong places, Roger had gone about his worthless activities trying to prove that he was wanted; needed even, and didn't need his father's approval. Needless to say, his reputation grew and many could be heard saying "you and your father are the same thing; no good!"

As Roger shook the memories away, he gathered the bag that he had brought with him for Mrs. Alleyne and made his way to the door. He hated reminiscing about his childhood. If he could erase it all tomorrow he would. The only things that he would let remain were his thoughts of Tricia Dessington.

CHAPTER 12

Tricia sat and stared at her mobile. Roger hadn't called her back as yet. She wondered what was taking the man so long that he wouldn't return her call. Maybe he was still angry with Elias about that morning; she knew she was. While she hadn't mentioned it again, she had been furious at his actions. She figured Elias would not have wanted her associating with the likes of Roger; he said so much when they had first started dating. But at that time Tricia had felt sorry for Roger. She knew a lot about his past. She was the only person he would talk to about his fears and dreams. They had been good friends but at a distance. No-one knew of their close friendship; Tricia feared no-one would understand. She was always the one to get to the root of things. She refused to take his behaviour at face value. There had to be a reason why Roger behaved this way and Tricia was determined to find out. At a church picnic, she saw Roger take off by himself in the direction of the flour mill. Taking a stroll in the opposite direction, Tricia diverted through a hidden track which led to the same mill. Her cadet days taught her most covered paths in Calvary. Fifteen minutes later, she saw his shadow around the far side of the limestone structure. Roger was sitting alone on the shaded grass. His face was a mask of pain. Without saying a word, Tricia sat beside Roger. She placed her hand around his shoulders and gave him a gentle squeeze. Soon, she felt his body shaking against her own. Roger was in tears. He had been overwhelmed by everything life had thrown at him. At such a tender age, he had been through so much. Granted, others had gone through worse than he had, but you can never tell anyone how to feel about their own circumstances. Roger quietly confided his problems in Tricia and she listened with an attentive ear. By the time he was finished, he felt much better and thanked her for listening. That was the beginning of a beautiful friendship. Tricia began to invite Roger to all the church events that came up; but Roger never really faced his problem head on. While he had gotten much off his chest that day, it still didn't fix the emptiness that he felt; and therefore Roger continued his undesirable activities. While it was easy for those who didn't know and therefore didn't understand to judge the young boy, Tricia focused her efforts on recovery. She was trying to show Roger there was a better life to be had than running from woman to woman without caution; but alas Roger had been so broken, he never changed his ways. This pushed Tricia away from Roger. She could only do so much for him, but he had to want to make the changes himself.

"I'm stepping out baby'" came Elias' voice from the back door. He had taken a long nap after lunch and was now making his way the Church Council meeting. Having seen the agenda for this evening, Tricia was certain Elias wouldn't have been back before midnight.

"No problem hun," was her lazy reply from upstairs. Tricia was stretched out across their bed, deep in the midst of a good book. The novel 'Caribbean Love Affair' by Jasmine Christine had caught her fancy and she was now engulfed in the controversy between Cassandra and her no- good boyfriend Andre. She too had already fallen in love with the other main character, Anderson MacDonald. Having been to Barbados several times before, she was able to picture each scene as they played out in the words of the author.

"Bzzz. Bzzz. Bzzz" Tricia's mobile phone vibrated somewhere between the sheets that she had somehow wrapped herself in. Sighing in slight annoyance, Tricia put down her book to search for the lost treasure. Guiding her hand beneath the pillows, she soon located the phone which had somehow lodged itself between the bed frame and the mattress. After looking at the caller ID, Tricia got even more annoyed when she didn't recognise the number. There were just some times that she rather be alone with a good book than to be troubled. "It may be someone in need" she cautioned herself. With that, she answered in a subdued manner.

"Hello," her soft voice travelled through the phone line and captured that of her caller. "Hello?" she asked once more. There had been no response on the line. Tricia, figuring the connection had been cut off, disconnected her handset and replaced it beside her. She took back up her book to continue where she had first left off.

"Bzzz, Bzzz, Bzzz… Bzzz, Bzzz, Bzzz…" The phone went off again; the caller the same. Tricia hesitated. Was this some kind of prank call? That slight annoyance now crept back into her voice.

"Hello!" she answered. Even though she had left her number earlier in the day and was waiting for this call, she hadn't been prepared for the caller.

"Hi Tee Tee. It's Roger." Tricia paused. She hadn't heard that nickname for so many years. It's what Roger used to call her; his warm cup of tea tea. Tea was a popular beverage in the islands. You could find most households partaking in the relaxing beverage morning and night. Starting your day with a warm cup of tea was a must, as was completing your night. The children more lovingly called for their tea tea before going to bed. Roger had thought it quite cute to shorten Tricia's name as such. No-one else had been allowed to call her that. He had made certain of it.

"Roger!" came Tricia's surprised exclamation.

"Did I call at a bad time? You sound surprised to hear me…" Roger didn't want any trouble with Elias. He had long moved past their differences, but he just didn't care for the man. He only acknowledged Elias' existence because he had married the woman of Roger's dreams.

"No… no it's not a bad time Roger that is quite fine. How are you doing?" Tricia smiled now. For some reason she was always comfortable with the young man. Not even in their teenage years could she say she was ever scared of him. He did have a quiet nature; you just had to know how to manage him.

"I am fine thanks," came his reply. "I was just a bit surprised that you had called that's all." Roger began to feel at ease. He didn't know what Tricia had wanted, neither did he really care. He still had a soft spot for her.

"I'm sorry I didn't call sooner but I had some errands to run." Tricia shook her head now as if Roger could see her.

"Not a problem my dear. I just wanted to chat with you for a bit." Get back to the task at hand Tricia. You called him for a reason; not to chitchat.

Roger was taken aback. What could she possibly have to say to him? They hadn't had a decent conversation in years except for the one that morning in the church yard. "Well, if your husband wasn't such a fierce protector I would invite you over for dinner so we could chat. But I wouldn't want to cause any trouble for you two."

Tricia blushed. She knew her husband's behaviour that morning was inexcusable. "Sorry about that Roger. Well he isn't here now so it shouldn't be a problem. I could join you at the hotel for dinner. He won't be back home for quite a bit anyway." Tricia closed the book as she spoke. What harm could dinner do? After all, they would be in the restaurant in the view of everyone. Not like she didn't have much deeper secrets from her husband in any case. Let's just add this one to the bucket.

"Ok. Well dinner at eight then?" Roger confirmed.

"Yes, eight would be fine."

"See you then my dear." With that the line went dead. Tricia had just over an hour to prepare herself. She opened the door to her walk in closet to see just which dress would be suitable for dinner tonight. Her clothes were always coordinated by colour. This made things much easier to find. Elias always joked about how anal she was about these things; but it was true. If ever she saw a blue piece of clothing mixed with her reds, there would be hell to pay. "Should I wear pink?" she wondered out loud. Why was she even getting so caught up with what she wore? It wasn't a date or anything. Tricia eventually opted for a glaring white knitted dress. It could pass for an intricate white knee length winter coat if one didn't know any better. The dress was accompanied by a white sash which fell perfectly to the right side of the hanger. "This is it," she thought. She picked out the perfect red accessories to go with her outfit including a lovely pair of high heeled red pumps. Once she was satisfied with her attire, Tricia made her way to the bath to get herself ready for dinner with Roger Duncan.

CHAPTER 13

Roger trekked down to the restaurant area a bit ahead of the agreed time. He wanted to pick the right location for their dinner. It couldn't be just anywhere. He wanted visibility, but just enough quiet so they could have a thorough conversation without being interrupted. Tricia still hadn't told him what she had wanted to talk about, and the more he thought about it, the less he cared. He chose to dress down for the occasion. He figured a suit would be too formal, and jeans may be too casual. He opted for Light khaki slacks and off white fitted buttoned shirt. He didn't wear a tie as outside was so warm, and opted to leave the first two buttons undone to allow better circulation. A Breitling Galactic 41 piece adorned his hand. Like Tricia, Roger liked nice things. He always believed he worked hard and he must enjoy his earnings so he had had no issue dishing out a few thousand dollars for the gorgeous work of art.

"Mr. Duncan…" Her voice trailed after she spoke as she willed him to acknowledge her presence. Roger's eyes moved from his wrist over to the direction where the voice came. Tricia had seen him in the corner by the medium sized palm tree and had made her way over to their table. Their waiter for the night assisted her with her chair as Roger rose respectfully.

"Mrs. Dessington…" Roger returned. He hated the name with every bone in his body; but it would have to do for now. They both settled into their seats as the waiter poured them each a glass of sparkling water and brought out the wine that Roger had pre- ordered. It was a bottle of Santa Rita Casa Real Cabernet Sauvignon from Maipo Valley Chile. Tricia loved that wine. It was one that could easily be found in her wine cooler at home. As the waiter walked away to give them time to look at their menus, Tricia took the opportunity to start her investigations.

"So, what have you been up to Roger?" Roger paused. He was still stunned that Tricia had wanted to see him furthermore to talk. He had sworn she had written him off so many years ago. But now, she was behaving as if he was a long lost friend that she needed to catch up with.

"Well," Roger started, "As you know, I moved to Canada some years ago and I'm an investment banker and analyst for a private company owned by two billionaires. I spend most of my time making money for them, and once they are happy, I am happy. The adrenaline keeps me going so I enjoy the job immensely. When I'm not making investments and trades, I'm usually out biking or working with the community youth group for fatherless boys. Kind of like a big brother programme."

Tricia was glad Roger had taken up the community work. Having gone through that stress in his own life, he was now offering himself to boys who were going through the same pains. At least they would have someone who understood them and knew all the signs when they were ready to give up. It's not that these boys were wayward; they just needed guidance. Tricia smiled. She knew that was a big step for Roger and she was proud of him. At her request, he continued to tell her about his 'little rascals' as he affectionately called them. She could see he enjoyed counselling the chaps. Whenever he spoke about one of them going through a rough patch, his own face sank as if it were his own son. There was one that he seemed especially fond of. Listening intently to his stories, Tricia figured it was because the boy was so much like him. The others were mostly the product of alcoholic dads or druggies. But this one was neglected by his dad who seemed to romp all over town. It was only after he started dating a girl in the neighbourhood the old man came forward and told him that was his sister. The boy and the girl had been distraught. At sixteen years old they had been the other's first love. They had even had sex a few times and the poor boy had been suicidal. It was by the grace of a form teacher that guided him to Roger who immediately got on the case. It took a while for him to get the boy past feeling worthless but Roger never relented. He called Timmy every single day to check on him and let him know that he cared. He even gave him free reign to turn up at his workplace whenever he needed to talk so that he would never feel alone. Things had tapered out over the last year but the boy was now like the son he never had. He promised him that even if he ever had children of his own he would never leave him out; and the boy trusted him. It had been hard coming to Grenada for the two weeks he was scheduled to be there, but Timmy had insisted. He didn't want Roger to feel he was a burden. Whenever Roger travelled, he always brought back a nice souvenir for Timmy which he always looked forward to. With a dead beat dad and a crack head mother, the boy had been glad he had a true friend and confident in Roger.

In coming to an end, Roger asked Tricia about her adventures since he had last seen her. Tricia began to describe her life as most people knew it; a successful accountant who adores the church. He asked her why she never had any children. Shrugging it off, she just chalked it up to both herself and her husband being too busy. It wasn't that she didn't want any children, but it just hadn't happened as yet. She too had been surprised that he hadn't gotten any kids of his own, but as he put it, he never found the right one. He didn't bother to tell her she was the only one he could see as the mother of his children.

Their appetizers soon arrived. Tricia had ordered her favourite; calamari. Roger had opted for the creamy seafood chowder. They both had a love for seafood, but it wasn't something that Tricia was allowed to participate in often. She usually had to wait for her trips overseas to eat seafood dishes. Elias was frightfully allergic so she couldn't even bring it into the house. She swore he would itch just by her saying the word shrimp! Their main was to be shared. They ordered a range of sushi pieces that came out on a large platter. The meal was simply divine. As they ate, the conversation continued. Roger casually mentioned that he had seen Tricia at the convention in Las Vegas some months ago, but she had been too far for him to reach out to her. At ease now that Roger had not been the one to send her that letter, Tricia allowed herself to enjoy the rest of dinner. They finished one and a half bottles of wine between the two of them during the course of the night and dinner lasted well close to four hours. Roger made Tricia laugh continuously. At times she could be seen with her head thrown back in a bout of laughter. She couldn't remember when last she had had such a good time. So much so that she almost didn't feel her phone vibrating on the edge of the table. Taking it up she started to frown when she saw the caller; it was her husband. He wasn't due home for another few hours so she knew he couldn't have been wondering where she was. She had been mistaken. Some nosy woman had left the hotel's restaurant and made her way to the church's compound where she knew the Bishop would be meeting. Tricia knew her well. Mrs.

Rawlings was a lovely woman; by stature, not by morals. Like Tricia, she was tall and trim. She had a neat waist, full breasts and hips and was always stylishly dressed. Her attitude however, left a lot to be desired. She was one dangerous force to be reckoned with. Mrs. Rawlings ruled her husband. The people of the church would often shake their head in pity as she was always seen ordering the poor lovesick man all over the place. They had been like chalk and cheese, but he thought he had won the world when she accepted his marriage proposal. Everyone but him knew that she was only after his money. The day that dried up she would be long gone. Even though she was married, Mrs. Rawlings had always had eyes for the Bishop. She couldn't see why he couldn't just leave Tricia to be with her. After all, she looked like Tricia, walked like Tricia and she had somehow perfected the woman's tone and mannerisms too. She had studied Tricia like a hawk. At one point Tricia had actually been flattered that someone would go to such lengths to be just like her. But when she realized that Mrs. Rawlings had had her eyes on her husband, Tricia had been furious. The woman had tried to befriend her in order to get close to Elias. It was only one day after Elias saw the woman having a drink with Tricia that he warned his wife about entertaining her. Days before she had shamelessly thrown herself at Elias during office hours, having gone there to talk to him about the problems in her marriage. Elias had been frank at that point. "The only problem I see in your marriage Mrs. Rawlings is you. You need to commit yourself to your husband and leave me alone!" Elias had had enough of her advances. And while he wasn't in Grenada every Sunday, he was there often enough for her to become a pest.

"How are you dear," Tricia answered her phone.

"Why didn't you tell me you were having dinner with Roger tonight? Why the secret Tricia?" Tricia's eyebrows shot into the air in surprise. She felt the heat begin to rise up the nape of her neck; she was annoyed. Since when did she have to tell him every single place she went? There were several occasions when both of them ended up in completely different locations than where they had first intended to be, so why was this innocent dinner a problem?

"When Roger called and asked me to dinner you had already gone. Did you want me to interrupt your meeting because of this?" Elias paused. He hated the fact that doubt had started to creep into his mind about his wife. It was something he had fought feverishly but he was losing the battle.

"No, I didn't expect you to disturb the meeting. I just thought you had made plans and didn't tell me anything that is all. When Mrs. Rawlins mentioned this to me I got upset.

"Since when do you let that woman get under your skin? Tricia asked in short tone.

"Since she reminded me that Roger had already taken one of my women away from me…" That devil! Not only had she gone to Elias to tell him Tricia was out with Roger, but she threw salt on the wound by reminding Elias he had been pretty incompetent at keeping his previous relationship from the grasps of Roger Duncan. This was her way of getting back at Elias for rejecting her. After dropping that bomb, Ms. Rawlings had walked out of the meeting with her chest puffed. The other persons of the 6 member committee just sat and stared as she pranced through the door, leaving Elias in shock and embarrassment. Tricia sat and listened to her husband recount the evening's happening. He then apologised for his jealousy and asked for her forgiveness. Tricia ended the call and returned to her dinner companion much more subdued than when the night first started. The call had put a damper on the joyous feeling she had not so long ago been enjoying.

Roger lowered his eyes to the dessert menu for the majority of the conversation. He couldn't tell what they had been talking about exactly, but he knew that whatever it was had upset Tricia. He knew the woman Mrs. Rawlings very well. In his younger days, she had been one of his conquests while she had been dating her now husband. Roger had counted his lucky stars that he had never been rich enough for the likes of her. He had moved in, taken what he wanted, and moved out. The sex hadn't even been all that great and he told her as much when she wouldn't stop sniffing around. On top of that she had known how Roger had felt about Tricia. That was the only reason she got with him to begin with. She wanted everything that Tricia had and more. She couldn't stand that Roger had loved Tricia and didn't love her. The mere mention of her name also upset Roger. He looked up now as Tricia ended her call.

"Are you ok?" he asked in hushed tones.

"I will be fine thanks," came the reply. Tricia didn't want to talk about it. It wasn't like she and Roger were bosom buddies or anything. She was just getting more and more frustrated with this marriage. Strangely enough Tricia didn't need to say a word. Roger could see her frustration written all over her face.

CHAPTER 14

∞

The two tried to continue the night but it was difficult to regain the previous hype that they had enjoyed.

"Look," started Roger. "Don't let foolish people get the better of you Tricia. Just always remember they walk among us. It will be difficult to avoid them."

Tricia knew he was right. She just had had her plate full already and didn't need the likes of Mrs. Rawlings to add fuel to the fire. "I guess you are right Roger."

For her final course, Tricia ordered a large brownie topped with nutmeg ice-cream and drizzled with white and dark chocolate. Roger opted for tiramisu as his dessert. They quietly continued their conversation, sharing their plans for the future. Short of the phone call that Tricia had received, it was a lovely night. Roger found out that Tricia had planned to attend the annual gospel festival in Vancouver Canada. This was always a massive event. While he lived in the heart of Toronto, he promised her he would go up to meet her there. Elias was slated to attend one of the church services as the guest preacher.

"I know your husband doesn't favour me much, but I am really not fazed by him. As far as I am concerned, if he is doing his job well as your husband, he shouldn't have to worry about you stepping out! You are one hell of a decent woman Tricia. What has him so jealous? Or am I the only one who gets under his skin?"

Tricia didn't know how to respond to this. She couldn't pinpoint exactly when this jealousy began to surface but she assured Roger that it started before she saw him this morning.

"I don't know to be honest…" Tricia trailed. "He has been somewhat over protective lately but I can't say when this all began."

"You didn't respond to whether or not he was being a good husband to you Tricia."

Tricia blushed uncontrollably. Could she trust Roger with her secret? No-one knew about the activities she got herself up to and it was beginning to become a burden. It wasn't that Elias was a bad husband at all. She enjoyed his company that's for sure. And she did enjoy being a wife to him; she just was sexually frustrated. That wasn't grounds to class him as a bad husband was it? No. Roger mustn't know her weakness. He may cause more problems in her relationship than she needed.

"Well I am still married to him aren't I?" she responded. Roger eyed her closely and Tricia lowered her gaze. He was no fool and he was more than certain now that Tricia Dessington had something to hide.

"So tell me about your sex life" he pushed gently. "If I remember correctly, you had quite a little spirit in you that night we were together." A sly grin crept across Roger's face now as Tricia's eyes shot up from her plate.

"Excuse me!?" Tricia began. "My sex life is none of your business Roger Duncan!" Roger could see he had touched a chord so he quickly back peddled.

"No need to get defensive doll. I just asked because mine is currently non-existent… but if you needed me to help you out there… you know I would gladly step up to the plate. I still have strong feelings for you Tricia. Your happiness is my only goal."

Tricia didn't know what to make of the offer. With Roger being in Canada on her next trip, should she indulge with the likes of him instead of hiring someone else? It wasn't like she wasn't attracted to him. Roger could see the wheels turning in Tricia's head. This woman was really considering having sex with him! He could tell by the way her eyes shifted from left to right as if searching for an answer.

"Look Roger, this is the first time I am seeing you in many years. Even if it were possible, I could not have sex with you. I love my husband dearly and I just couldn't do that to him." Do what exactly she thought. Hadn't she already broken the oath of marriage by sleeping with other men? Roger Duncan was different. He wasn't just another man; he was the thorn in Elias' side. If she did something like that it would surely kill him. No. She would stick to her routine. She would hire someone to do that job.

The organisers of the gospel fest had provided accommodation for the visiting priests in one of the church's community centres. Since there was lots of work to be done, they had opted to keep the priests close by. Tricia had already told Elias she wasn't going to be sleeping on a cot for a week. He wasn't even going to be available to keep her company. Instead, she chose to spend her nights in a hotel and he was to join her after his duties were done. They would spend another week together as a little vacation and actually look to do some sightseeing in Vancouver before they returned to Calvary Isle.

"Well, I am just letting you know how I feel. I will respect your decision. But know this Tricia, if ever you give me the green light, married or not, I will make love to you like you have never experienced before!"

The words sent a shiver down Tricia's spine. She looked straight into Roger's eyes when he said this. His hand moved to cover her own and she knew he had been dead serious about his proposal.

Tricia gave a slight nod in acknowledgement. There was no confirmation on her end, but what Roger received had been enough. Tricia was too lovely a lady to be depressed about anything and Roger could see in her face that something was troubling her.

They quietly finished up dessert and said their goodbyes. Roger walked Tricia to her vehicle in the hotel's car park. As she unlocked her door, Tricia paused.

"Have you ever written me a letter Mr. Duncan?" The strange question threw Roger off guard.

"Yes, I have… I have written you a letter Tricia. But I never had the guts to send it so how do you know about my love letter?" Ignoring his question, Tricia asked another one of her own.

"Why had you never delivered it to me then?" Roger paused. To answer this question would mean to completely open up to Tricia about his feeling for her. He didn't know if he would have been able to handle her rejection again.

"I couldn't Tricia" came his soft but firm reply. Tricia grew even more curious about this letter that Roger hadn't sent.

"But why? Was it a bad letter?" Roger began to shake his head slowly. Tricia just didn't get it did she. He had been so in love with her that he couldn't afford for her to crush him. He had been hurt one too many times as a child and he would have rather that she not know how he felt than for him to tell her and she fully reject his advances. Roger gave her a piercing stare now. They weren't children anymore. He was a grown man with a fruitful career and she too had done much for herself over the years. They had both matured well past their teenage years so maybe she would understand his feelings just a bit better.

"I didn't send it because I had been too in love with you Tricia," Roger started. "If I had sent it to you, and had you not replied, I would have surely taken my life."

Tricia nodded. She understood completely. Roger couldn't afford for anyone to hurt him again; especially her. She had known he had liked her, but to hear him admit to loving her melted Tricia's heart. She smiled. "Do you still have the letter?"

Roger bowed his head; slightly embarrassed. He had indeed kept the letter over the years. He pulled it out every so often and read and reread it. He knew each line by heart. Now as a grown man, he sometimes wondered what ever made him write those mushy words. Raising one eyebrow, Roger gave Tricia a sceptical look. "Do you want to see it?"

Tricia was a romantic by heart. She would have loved to have read that letter that Roger had penned. She began to nod profusely as she felt the heat begin to rise to her cheeks. She would also keep this letter in her secret drawer.

It definitely wasn't Roger who had sent her the nasty mail. She had felt certain about this. He couldn't hurt her even if he tried. Without another word Tricia placed a gentle kiss on Roger's cheek. She felt the tension build between the two of them. The car-park was deserted so no one would have been there to see anything happen between the two of them; not that Roger cared. He instinctively wrapped his hands around Tricia's waist and dragged her closer to his body. Hugging her closely, he buried his face in the curve of her neck. She smelt so good. Tricia's own arms reached up and wound their way around Roger's broad shoulders. She felt his face shift now as he began to place soft butterfly kisses along the path to her ear. Tricia felt her body begin to dissolve. Roger oozed sex and she knew now how badly he wanted her. The close embrace gave her the proximity to feel his penis begin to swell in his pants. Lord knows it had been a few weeks since she had a good work over. Tricia pressed her body now onto his and Roger captured her earlobe in his mouth. She could feel his breath as it blew on the few loose strands of hair that had eased their way out of her bun. Her knees buckled as he extended his tongue now into the depth of her ear. This always weakened Tricia as her ears were the most sensitive part of her body. As he felt her weight drop slightly, Roger placed his hand on her rounded bottom and squeezed. A soft moan involuntarily escaped Tricia's lips as the air thickened around them. She could feel the moistness begin to form between her legs as Roger abused her neck and ear interchangeably. She could feel his body stiffen now as he leaned her against the closed car door and rubbed his manhood against her pelvis. Stopping only a moment to look into her eyes, Tricia saw Roger's burning desire to make love to her. He placed his forehead onto hers; his eyes searching for her consent. Before she could resist his tongue snaked its way into her waiting mouth. The kiss was hot and ferocious. Tricia now grabbed the back of Roger's neck and he crushed her lips with his own. She was returning his kiss with as much energy as he brought to her.

"Let me make love to you Tricia. Please. Let me make love to you. I know that you want me to. I can feel it baby!"

Tricia tried to regain her composure, but Roger kissed her again as she began to shake her head. She was trying to say no but her body was saying yes! Roger released her waist now and slipped one hand beneath her dress. Luckily, the only car space that had been available that night was around the back of the hotel. No-one would be passing there at this hour. Between the wine and both their desire for each other, it was almost the best scene for disaster. Roger gently squeezed her vagina; feeling her wetness begin to seep through. The action caused Tricia to wine in the palm of his hand. She raised her right leg slightly to give him more access to her.

"This pussy always got wet for me didn't it?" Roger asked the question as Tricia's head fell back against the car. She couldn't think straight. This was proving to be a big mistake. Roger planted kisses along her exposed neck; nibbling along the way. He was driving Tricia wild. It had been quite a while for him as well. He just hadn't been enticed by the thought of any woman recently and so he kept himself busy to fill the void. Now however, Tricia Dessington was sending him back to the place he thought he had long buried. He could feel the animal in him trying to escape as Tricia softly whispered his name. He pushed the lining of her panty one side now as he began to caress her bare flesh. He wanted to take her to his room but Tricia shook her head. She was trying to fight the feeling as best as she could but she still had a soft spot for Roger. Not about to lose momentum, Roger dropped to his knees before Tricia could protest. Placing her heeled foot on top of his shoulder, Roger buried his face in her soft dew. Tricia cried out in pleasure. Roger sucked gently on her clit as Tricia's knees weakened some more. Using pure brute strength now, Roger placed the other heeled foot on his free shoulder and spread her knees further apart. You would not believe he had just had such a filling meal the way he ate Tricia. Licking and sucking was all he needed to bring her to her demise. Tricia came into his mouth, holding his head as she felt the fluid rush through her core. Roger gladly received every drop that Tricia had to offer. He would eat her every day if she allowed him. She had such a wonderful taste. As she came down from her high, Roger kissed the inside of her thighs and squeezed her ass. Looking up with a face of gratitude, he said to her "There is much more where that came from Mrs. Dessington. Don't you ever forget that."

Tricia let her head fall back onto the top of the car as Roger assisted her to her feet. Her cravings and desires were getting out of hand and she needed to put a stop to this before it caused her to lose her marriage.

CHAPTER 15

Tricia opened her back door and entered the quiet house. It was still early for Elias to return home so she had about an hour to freshen up before he arrived. She had left soon after Roger helped her into her car. He had asked her to wait in the lobby just a few moments while he ran to his room to collect the letter. She was surprised that he still had it furthermore had brought it back home with him. He used to take it everywhere; just in case he ever got the courage to post it. Now, no postage was necessary. Tricia had stared at the olive green envelope for a few seconds before she accepted the letter. Olive green was her favourite colour and Roger remembered that; this touched her. Though the letter showed age, one could tell that it had been kept under pristine conditions. Roger told her that he kept it in a large bible his mother had given to him just before she had gone into the hospital. He kept that and a picture of himself and his mom in the bible. The yellow spots on the paper told Tricia that he had indeed written the letter some time ago. She was eager to read its contents but she knew she needed to get out of his sight before worst occurred.

On the drive home Tricia fixated on what had just occurred in the car park. On one end she felt very guilty as she knew Elias would have hit the roof had he found out. He probably would have divorced her on the spot! On the other hand she had never felt that level of passion from Elias. Marriage was more than just eating meals and having fellowship together. The Lord made the union of marriage for physical enjoyment as well. And this part was seriously lacking in her eyes. It was also beginning to affect the other aspects of her marriage. Sometimes, because of her frustrations, Tricia didn't feel to talk to Elias. Sometimes she didn't feel to go anywhere with him. Some days she would just get about her duties without saying ten words to him. What's the point? The intimacy wasn't there. She would watch other couples hug and give soft pecks in adoration. None of this she got anymore. It all dwindled over the years. It was almost a clinically functioning marriage. They moved well together. They looked good together. Ate, drank and worshiped together. But when it came to intimacy, it didn't exist. The men that Tricia hired had been more into her than her own husband. A few of them even came prematurely having been so excited to make love to her. They had all been at her beck and call. None had left regretting having passed Tricia's way. Tricia too was immensely satisfied. Her only regret being that it wasn't the man whom she had married before God that was pleasuring her.

Retreating to her favourite spot in the living-room, Tricia settled herself into the big armchair with her letter. Even though it had been written years before, the thought of what was enclosed in that letter caused butterflies in her stomach. She ran her fingers over the tough envelope. It was a high quality paper that made the folded beauty. Inside, Tricia could see the letter was written on a similar high quality paper. She removed the letter from the pocket and eyed it curiously. The letter had been carefully handwritten; not even typed. It had been addressed to 'My Beautiful Tee Tee'. Tricia hadn't been fully prepared for the words that followed:

"Dear Tricia,

I am so unsure of how you would receive this; but I will write it anyway. Just know that every word that I place in this letter is right from my heart. I want you to know exactly how I feel about you. You know I am not one of many words, but there is something about you that made me want to express my true feelings. It's been a while now since I noticed your beauty; and I must admit, I am captivated. It is not just your physical attributes which throws me in awe, but your mental capabilities as well. You are a strong woman Tee Tee; not like some of these weak minded women in this country. You don't take advantage of anyone and you are quick to forgive. You truly are a gem. I watched you working with those homeless guys and the way they cling to you as if you are their saviour. Young children look up to you and many of the girls can be heard praising you and your ways. The old, the young, the rich and the poor all had one thing in common; they loved you Tricia. To see the impact you make on so many lives makes me want to get close to you as I know you are the only one that could heal my pain.

Your body also began to blossom like none that I have ever laid eyes on. I know it is wrong to lust after you but I can't help myself. Many nights I sit in a rage because you wouldn't give me the time of day. You are a true friend to me every time I need one. I am sorry that I can't be a better man for you. No one will ever love you as much as I do Tricia; that is for certain. I so want to make love to you to show you exactly how I feel. These other women mean nothing to me and I would give it all up just for a chance to be with you. Just show me a sign that you and I can be together, and everything that exists now will be no more. I'll never give up on you Tee Tee. I swear I'll love you forever.

Love Always
Roger"

Tricia rubbed the leaf of paper between her fingers. She read and reread that letter as the words gave her life. Roger had not just wanted her body; he wanted every inch of her being. His words had been powerful. He appreciated Tricia and wanted to let her know how he felt. Tricia figured this was the best way Roger knew how. He really never spoke much to the people in the community; he just went about his business in a quiet manner. It was usually because of boasting women that his business even got onto the streets. The girls used to flock for his attention. He was a delicious piece of eye candy to be honest.

Tricia heard the door close in the still of the night. Elias must have gotten home by now. Quickly, she replaced the letter in its envelope and hurried to her desk in the kitchen. No sooner had she dropped the letter into the little slot, than Elias come through the kitchen calling her name. Tricia froze.

"Are you ok Tricia?" Elias asked concerned.

"Yes. Yes I am thanks" Tricia replied; hurriedly moving away from the desk. "I was waiting for you to return home. Let's go to bed Elias."

Elias had come home to apologise. That wicked woman had been furious after he didn't retaliate at her "good" news. She had expected at least a little scene in the yard when she mentioned that Tricia was having dinner with his "rival". She had watched closely that morning as Elias had rushed to Tricia's side when seeing her talking to Roger. The jealousy was real and Mrs. Rawlings had plotted to get in between them one way or the other. When she and her girlfriends had decided to go to Hilton for drinks, and she saw the cosy couple having such a blast, she had behaved as if she had won the lottery! This was finally it she thought. Elias will hit the roof when he hears this! She quickly ended her drink and excused herself from the gathering to make her way to the church. Elias, however, just stared at her in disbelief. He apologised to the rest of the committee for the outburst and carried on until the scheduled break. It was then that he called Tricia to find out what exactly was going on.

Now, Tricia just wanted to withdraw to her room. She didn't want to talk to Elias or hear about the meeting. She didn't want anything to cloud her mind at this point. She was tired. All Tricia wanted was to get some rest. As she lay in their bed, she couldn't help but recount the activities earlier that night. Roger Duncan was treading a very dangerous path.

CHAPTER 16

The sun streamed through the partially open curtain. Tricia stretched lazily as her body tried to come to grips with having to wake up. Turning slightly, she noticed that Elias was not in his usual spot beside her in the bed. That was odd. Tricia usually had to drag him out of bed every morning. Blinking now to adjust her eyes to the brightness of the room, she glanced around trying to see where he might have gone to. Realizing she couldn't hear him moving about in the bathroom, Tricia got up and put on her robe to set off downstairs. Maybe he had gone to start breakfast. She doubted this. Elias never even boiled himself a cup of tea! As she stepped onto the teak wooden floor of their spacious living room, Tricia noticed her husband was sitting in the large sofa with his back to her. It was strange to see him here this early in the morning. A quick glance on the clock told her it was 5:30 AM. This was definitely too early for him to be going over his Sunday notes. What could he be doing over there? Quietly she stepped closer. She didn't want to disturb him if it was frightfully important, but when she looked over his shoulder, she realized he was just sitting and staring into space. Gently, she put her hand on the nape of his neck.

"Elias?" Elias' body jerked. Was that a cringe she felt? "Is something wrong hun?" Elias glanced over his right shoulder in the direction of where her voice was coming from. He didn't fully turn around; neither did he fully acknowledge her. Mechanically, his head turned right back to where it had originally started without so much as a word escaping his lips. Tricia was baffled. This type of behaviour from Elias was foreign to her. She hastily rounded the sofa to come face to face with her husband. Tricia paused as she now tried to understand the expression etched on his face. His elbows were propped forward on his knees and his hands joined at the fingertips as if in deep thought. His chin was propped on his touching fingertips.

"Elias...?" Elias didn't look up from his position. Tricia noticed his eyes had been red as if he had either been crying or from lack of sleep. From the angle at which he held his head she couldn't be entirely sure.

"What on earth is wrong dear?" she asked more concerned now than anything else.

"You tell me Tricia" came the vague and weary reply. Tricia was confused. How could she answer the question?

"I don't understand Elias? What do you want me to say?" Tricia paused. If he was looking to her for answers then something else must be going on and something that she was sure she wouldn't like! Elias glanced up at his wife. His eyes looked swollen. His hair was uncombed and this made him look older than his tender age. The stubble from his beard still adorned his jaws as he was yet to shave for the morning. There was a pain engraved on Elias' face that Tricia couldn't comprehend. What could be troubling him so much? "Is this about dinner last night? I thought we had already discussed this?"

Elias' expression didn't change. He stared now deep into his wife's eyes; not sure how exactly this conversation would turn out. He took a deep breath and opened his mouth to say something. Nothing came out. He closed his lips and began to shake his head.

"Oh for crying out loud Elias, tell me what is going on!" Tricia was becoming impatient. Her husband looked as if he had been hit by a truck and was trying to gather the little pieces off the street.

"What happened last night Tricia?" Tricia took a step back. Elias shifted his gaze to the clock on the wall; almost willing the hands to fly back in time and erase this entire mess.

"What do you mean Elias?" she asked cautiously.

Elias could feel the anger building inside of him again. It was the reason he had left their room to begin with. He couldn't have stayed another minute in the same room as her. Tricia's face dropped. Elias couldn't have known about the episode in the car park; could he?

"I don't understand what you are asking me Elias. I went to dinner with Roger at the Hilton. You know this already!"

Elias' eyes moved back to his wife's face. "And after...?" The question caused Tricia's legs to feel weak. She promptly took a seat right opposite her husband. Elias could see her eyes searching; as if trying to understand what he was trying to get at.

Tricia's counsellor training shifted into gear. You are never to expose your views to the one being counselled by showing facial expression. The problem was that Elias wasn't a client; he was her husband.

"And after what Elias? We had dinner and I came home. Where is all of this coming from and why are you questioning me all of a sudden?"

She hadn't exactly told a lie. It wasn't like she went to his room or anything. He couldn't possibly know about anything else so she would hold her ground. Tricia started to become annoyed.

"You don't trust me Elias?" she asked. Elias' jaws clenched. He had been quite fine until the likes of Roger Duncan turned up; or at least he fooled himself of such. The truth was, since that night that he realized how much his wife liked wild sex, he grew quite aware of the lack of intimacy in his own relationship. He also experienced a few things after that episode but he chose to ignore them to keep his sanity; but Roger Duncan was more than Elias could bear. It wasn't that he didn't find his wife attractive; he just wasn't that type of guy. Elias began his response slowly.

"It isn't that I don't trust you Tricia, but you have been giving me more indications in the last few months that I may not be enough of the man that you need." Elias spoke cautiously trying to maintain his composure.

"What do you mean? I have never said this to you! Why would you feel inadequate?" It wasn't that he was lying, but Tricia had been careful to avoid any such conversation with him in case she had hurt his feelings.

"No... you are right...you have never said this to me, but your actions last night spoke volumes!" Tricia went pale. So he did know about last night! But how? Did he leave the church and come up there to see her? Should she deny everything? Tricia was a mess. Tears began to roll down her face now as the tension between them thickened. She didn't respond; there was nothing left for her to say. Somehow Elias had found out about her and Roger in that car-park. How could she have been so stupid and careless?

"Did... did he make love to you Tricia?" The question jolted Tricia out of her thoughts. Something wasn't right. What did he mean make love to her? What was he talking about now? Something wasn't adding up.

"When I left the restaurant I went straight to the car-park Elias. There was no love making last night... what is this all about?" Tricia was a little more confident now. The mere fact that he had asked that question meant that he hadn't seen them; but something had occurred last night to make her husband question her dedication and loyalty to their marriage.

Elias' eyes pierced her own as Tricia stood her ground. She knew she had done wrong, but there was no way Elias knew what Roger and she had gotten up to last night. The thought of it caused moisture to form between her legs again. Tricia shifted her eyes before Elias could notice the change in her facial expression.

"I am getting pretty weary of you and this jealousy Elias. Where is this all coming from all of a sudden?!" Tricia's voice grew sterner with each word. "Recently you have been behaving as if you cannot trust me around men! I travel the world on your behalf; are you telling me that you are concerned every time I leave your eyesight?" A slight form of reverse psychology couldn't hurt. Let's get the focus off of me for a bit Tricia figured.

"No... I am not concerned every time you leave my side Tricia, that is preposterous... but should I be?" Curve ball! Tricia snickered a bit but nothing about this conversation was funny. She rose from her seat, and began to make her way to the kitchen.

"I have had enough of this foolishness Elias! I am too old to be playing games, and I certainly am allowed to have dinner in public places if I wish. Get a grip of yourself if you want this marriage to continue on the same path it has been on for the past few years!" With that, Tricia turned to walk towards the kitchen.

"You cried out his name..." a choked whisper escaped Elias' lips.

"What did you say?"

"Much stronger now, Elias repeated his statement. "You called out his name Tricia...last night... in our bed... you called Roger's name..."

Tricia spun around to face her husband's back again. He didn't turn to face her. Instead, he placed his forehead on his pointed fingertips and waited. Elias expected the worst. The type of pleasure that he had heard Roger was capable of giving, he was sure the man had finally gotten his hands on his wife. And who could blame her? It was clearly what she wanted!

Tricia didn't know when her jaws had dropped open. The only thing worse than physical infidelity, was emotional infidelity.

"You must have been mistaken Elias... that is impossible!"

Elias flew out of the sofa now to a standing position. In one fluid movement he spun around to face his wife. "Really Tricia! Do you take me for some kind of fool?!"

Tricia stumbled back by the force of his voice. Elias was angry; there was no hiding that. He had kept his cool the entire time, but the mere fact that she was suggesting that he might be somewhat crazy was just too much.

"I was implying no such thing Elias! I just do not understand why I would be calling out Roger's name in my sleep!" Tricia knew oh too well but she had to deny it. There was no way she would let her world crumble now; not at this point. They hadn't even had sex for crying out loud! Not that the little encounter they had was not enough to merit Elias' anger, but she just didn't understand what had happened last night.

Elias's face showed glaring sarcasm now. "The way you were calling his name and grinding on the bed didn't tell me that you have no idea Tricia! As a matter of fact, the way you touched yourself and moaned convinced me something must have happened!"

"Convinced you?!" Tricia now filled with anger. "You have already convinced yourself that I cheated on you before you even spoke to me!"

"Can you blame me Tricia?! Can you really say you blame me?! I know that man! I know him very well! He would do anything to get his filthy paws on you! And you...my wife... is in MY bed... OUR bed... enjoying him pleasuring you! How do you think I should behave Tricia? You tell me!" Tricia was lost for words. Elias was right. It could not have been a good experience for him to watch her writhe with pleasure and calling out another man's name; especially Roger Duncan's.

"Look Elias... I must have been dreaming... that is all."

"Dreaming about another man Tricia? Dreaming about Roger Duncan?! Am I not enough man for you Tricia? Again I ask!" Tricia didn't know how to answer that question. She never had sex with Roger, but the few bits she had experienced were a hell of a lot more pleasure than she ever got from Elias! But how could she tell the man she married this? Tricia shook her head. Tears flowed rivers down her face now. He didn't understand how hard it was for her; how frustrated she had been all these years! And in trying to be respectful towards his feelings she had woven a basket of deceit; a second life so that she could have the sexual satisfaction she needed. She hadn't intended to get involved with Roger last night and she certainly didn't plan for it to go any further in the future. How could she get her husband to give her the loving that she wanted from him? She would give it all up in an instant if Elias would only cater to her needs.

"Elias, I do not know what to say to you but to tell you the truth. Roger and I did not have sex last night. Actually, we have never had sex and I have no plans to have sex with the man. I cannot control my dreams and I am very sorry that they have offended you. If I could have controlled them, I would have. I told you one time about my dream of riding a unicorn in the clouds and you laughed at me. It is the same thing Elias. I cannot explain it nor can I control it, it just happened. And for that I am sorry that it has hurt you to this extent." Nothing Tricia said had been a lie. She couldn't control her dreams now could she? And she certainly didn't have sex with Roger. There was nothing left to say at this point. They would just have to try to get past this as best as they could.

CHAPTER 17

The following weeks were torturous. Roger had long gone back to Canada and Elias was barely speaking to his wife. In his mind, he was still trying to come to grips with what had happened that night. The devil was well at work with making him doubt Tricia but he knew she had never lied to him before; not to say that there wouldn't have been a first time. Elias knew Tricia was dedicated to their marriage but Roger Duncan had been nothing but bad news in his life. Lately, Elias found himself questioning many things about Tricia. As more doubt crept into his mind, he had begun watching her more closely. Trying to be discrete, Elias began peeping behind her to see how long she took to do certain things. He had also put certain mechanisms in place for the times she wasn't in his eyesight. It was 3 hours for her weekly shopping which included the drive to and from the supermarket. Elias had offered to take this trip with her several times so he could time this himself. It took her approximately an hour and a half to cook for the less fortunate and dish out the food to be collected. Once he thought she should be finished, he would call and inquire about how it went. Tricia usually gave him a run for run of any hiccups she may have encountered during the day. He always told her to get some rest once the food was collected as he wasn't sure when he would be coming home for lunch. Though he spent his mornings at the church, he would be home in the evenings until his meetings in the night. He never set a specific time for lunch so Tricia wouldn't have had any space to get up to mischief. He hated how he had become but he thought it was necessary. Although he went to great lengths to monitor his wife, he knew he couldn't be with her every step of the way.

Tricia went about her daily tasks quietly. It had been weeks since she had ruffled Elias' feathers and her husband still wasn't himself. Though they slept in the same bed every night, there was a massive space between the two of them. Conversations had become near non-existent. Tricia cooked and went about her wifely duties without much fuss and responded to Elias whenever he thought he should say something to her. The way they were living at this point depressed Tricia. It was the very thing she had hoped to avoid. She worked all her life to be happy; this was not a very happy time for the couple. Roger had texted her to let her know he had gotten back home safely. Tricia opened up to Roger and told him what had happened that night and how Elias had responded. Roger apologised for causing any problems, but, he told her he was not sorry for pleasing her. Tricia had mixed emotions about the entire thing. She knew she should have cut Roger off right there and then but she couldn't find it in herself to do this; he gave her the attention she craved. They continued talking to each other over mobile messaging during this uncomfortable period. Roger hated the fact that Tricia was so depressed about her marriage and he figured there must still be a piece to the missing puzzle; from both ends. Yes, Elias had every right to be upset about what he had heard, but if he really trusted his wife, he should have gotten over this by now. Men don't tend to hold grudges for over a month! And Tricia, yes she had done wrong, but it was a dream; there was nothing she could do about it. Roger was sure there was more to the situation than meets the eye but he wasn't in the best position to pry any further information from Tricia being so many miles away. All he could do was try to be the friend that Tricia had been to him during his times of need. Had Roger had his way, he would have given the stupid man something to be upset about. If only Elias knew the things Roger would have loved to do to his wife that night; that night and every night for the rest of her life! The man was right to be guarded. While Roger hadn't set out to trouble Tricia, he had not been able to help himself. The woman had been so damn sexy in that outfit. He had noticed her plump ass protruding through the thick cloth as he had walked her to her car that night. Roger did all in his power not to reach forward and just grab the wonderful piece of art. He could tell she had worn a thong by the way each cheek trembled as she walked. Lord, this woman was not good for any man's heart. By the time they had reached the vehicle, Roger had just wanted to cop a little squeeze; nothing more. When he hugged her and felt her body respond to his, he knew he was going over the edge. Tricia Dessington wanted every minute of what happened that night. She couldn't deny that. The man hadn't forced himself on her for crying out loud. She returned his kiss just as hungrily as he had given her. Tricia wanted the affection he had shown her; needed it even, and Roger wasn't about to stop. He already made up in his mind he may end up in hell for all the things he had gotten himself into in life. He tried to turn his life around but Tricia has always been his weakness. As she wined her pelvis against him when he grabbed her ass, Roger knew he was giving her exactly what she wanted. She had moaned, not complained. That woman was horny and Roger had serviced her. When he tasted her they both had seen a piece of heaven. Tricia grabbed his head willing him to go deeper into her; and Roger obliged her. This couldn't be pinned on him damn it! Your wife wanted this Elias! Roger made himself a promise that as long as Tricia would have him; he was going to do right by her. These past few weeks they had gotten closer as a result of the entire thing. If that foolish man thought he was going to give up on the love of his life, he had another thing coming. Roger Duncan was going to fight for Tricia's heart. It was up to Elias to ensure that he didn't win that fight.

CHAPTER 18

The trip to Canada was around the corner. Elias still was not speaking to Tricia so she hadn't made any arrangements to be there. Not wanting to seem too eager to go, Tricia didn't say anything about it to Elias.

"Are you still going to Canada?" Elias eyed Tricia steadily. He was upset that she didn't seem to be noticing the fact that he wasn't really speaking to her; it was as if she didn't care anymore. She went about her days as if nothing had happened. While she returned his silence with equal vibrancy, Tricia didn't reach out to Elias to make amends. What was he expecting her to say exactly? There was nothing that she could do really. He was beginning to feel like a heel for the way he was treating her. Elias still loved his wife and he knew she had told him the truth; she didn't have sex with Roger. That much he believed. It still choked him to think about her dreaming about the man. He literally felt a constant pain in his chest for days after that episode. Tricia had shown concern earlier on, but in the latter days she just ignored him as he did her. They both moved about the house as if the other didn't exist; luckily it hadn't been a mansion or they might not have ever seen each other again!

Tricia was surprised that Elias spoke to her but she didn't show it. Without raising her eyes from the newspaper she had been reading at breakfast, she asked "am I still required to go?"

Elias hated this. If it was one thing that he and Tricia did well before, it was talking. Now, his wife resorted to checking and replying to emails while he ate lunch and reading the newspaper each morning at breakfast. He wasn't even sure if she ate dinner as by the time he came home she would already be put up in bed on her iPad. His food would be waiting for him on the table as customary.

"No… it is not a requirement… so I am not forcing you to go. I just remember that you had previously spoken about accompanying me and it usually is expected that the wives of the Bishops turn up."

Tricia was not in the mood to mingle with "the wives of the Bishops" to be quite honest. Lately, she just didn't care about that aspect of her ministerial duties. There had been two events that Elias was invited to since the argument that he had been unable to attend; Tricia had stayed home. Elias had not asked her to attend on his behalf either. Tricia didn't know how long this would go on, but what she did know is that if it went on much longer she would be finding herself a job to occupy her time. There was no way she would be sitting down twiddling her thumbs days on end. Giving up her job to do the Lord's work was one thing, but if Elias didn't plan to use her anymore, she would find a corporation who did.

"Well, if you would like me to attend I am sure you would state such. If not, I do not need to go to Canada. It is your event so you let me know and I would make myself available."

Elias closed his eyes. He hadn't realized how much they had drifted apart over the years. This one situation opened so many cans of worms; more than he knew how to deal with. Elias looked over his wife now. She was almost like a stranger living under the same roof. When was the last time he even held that woman in his arms? He can't say when last he had kissed her lips, or even simply held hands with her. The only time they touched was through passing, yet he boasted about his wife every time he got into the pulpit. Elias' depression deepened. Of course he still loved his wife, but he hadn't shown her any love in quite some time. Here it was that Tricia had given up everything for him, and dedicated her life to making him comfortable, yet he doesn't show the woman any affection. Tricia received more flowers and gifts from members of the church than she did her own husband. When last had they gone out to dinner together? Or even just out to the country for a drive. These were things they used to do while they were courting, now, they didn't exist anymore. Tricia just accepted life as it came. She must be bored being his wife, he was almost sure of it.

"I want you to go Tricia. You deserve to relax." Tricia placed the newspaper on the table and peered over her reading glasses.

"I am not going anywhere where you don't think you could trust me Elias. I am safe right here. And besides, roaming calls would cost you quite a bit if we both were up in Canada." Tricia took back up her paper with an attitude and continued to read. Elias' eyebrows knotted. Since when was Tricia concerned about roaming charges?

"Come again?" he asked.

"You heard me!" Tricia put back down the paper again with a thud. "You don't think I realized you call me at the same time each day? Checking to see if I'm up to something? I wouldn't want you to run up a nasty bill while up there my dear. You go on to Canada. I will spend my time liming with Mrs. Rawlings so you can get a play by play report on my activities when you return." She picked the paper back up with a force.

Elias' face turned red with embarrassment. He didn't realize Tricia had noticed. Clearly he wasn't as good at it as he thought, yet she never said a word. Tricia had always hated conflict and just moved about her business.

"I want you to go Tricia." Tricia nodded. As usual, she wasn't in the mood to converse. Most of her conversations now took place on her smartphone via messages to Roger. While they had been always decent conversations, Tricia found herself looking forward to spending that quality time with someone who actually cared for her.

"Ok." Tricia mumbled. She didn't have anything further to say. If he wanted her to go she would go as a dutiful wife would do.

"Look Tricia, I hate how things have become between us. I am sorry. I realize how wrong I have been about you and I feel stupid for ever doubting you. Please forgive me."

Tricia didn't know what to say. Elias had not been completely at fault in this entire thing. She had done wrong and she knew it. What she didn't do was bring this drama into their marriage. She still blamed Elias for her straying ways anyway.

"I forgive you Elias." It didn't make any sense drawing this out any further or trying to complicate things with explanations. Elias got up and placed a kiss on Tricia's cheek. It was the closest they had been in months.

Later that night, Tricia told Roger what had happened. Though he didn't like it one bit, he was glad Tricia felt a little better. He was more her friend now than anything else. At this rate, this was all he would ever be.

CHAPTER 19

Tricia packed her suitcases to take on the trip. It was the first time she would be leaving without a piece of lingerie. While she had a week alone before Elias joined her at their hotel, she didn't feel to organise any of her special meetings. The guilt was still taking a toll on her. Maybe if she tried again he would be more receptive. Tricia doubted this would be the case. She was between a rock and a hard place. On one end she wanted to be the faithful wife, on the other, her husband was awful at sex. As Tricia closed the suitcase, Elias came up behind her and squeezed her in a hug. Elias was being very loving lately. It was a strange feeling to have him holding her so regularly and Tricia still jumped whenever it occurred. This confused Tricia more and more each day. She had become so accustomed to being alone in this marriage. Then, there was her growing friendship with Roger. Now, Elias was trying to have conversations and take her out on dates. It was beginning to be too much. Wasn't this what you had wanted Tricia? She usually chastised herself when she didn't feel to be with her husband. She didn't realize how disconnected she had become in this marriage. Spinning her around, Elias planted a firm kiss on her lips.

"All set my dear?"

"I believe so," Tricia returned.

"You don't sound so excited about this trip…" Elias was concerned. He had expected Tricia to be elated at the thought of them spending some alone time together. No work, no needy people, no church activities, just the two of them. The reality is Tricia didn't have a clue what she would do with her husband during that free week! She was so accustomed just going about her daily duties that she knew she would feel like a fish out of water.

"It's not that I'm not excited dear, I guess I am still shaken by all that had happened." It was the excuse she used for everything now the past week and a half. Elias had immediately set about making her arrangements for the trip. He put her up in one of the best rooms in the hotel and bought her a first class ticket right beside himself. He booked several adventures over the course of the time they would be there. Even though the first week was dedicated to his work, that second week he had planned to show his wife how much he loved and appreciated her.

"I guess I will come around sooner or later dear. I am still trying to pull myself together." Elias hoped it would be sooner rather than later.

On the way to the airport, Tricia sat quietly in the passenger seat fiddling with her phone. Through the corner of his eye Elias could see her smiling shyly as if the recipient could see her face.

"Who, pray tell, has my wife so jovial this morning?" Tricia looked up from the handset and glanced over to Elias. There was no way she could tell him she had been talking to Roger all morning. Roger was actually trying to cheer her up about the trip. For some reason Tricia was dreading this trip. It was as if all the pent up depression came crashing down on her shoulders these last few days. She hadn't realized how unhappy she had really been. She had spent most of her time at other people's beck and call and therefore never took full stock of how her marriage was affecting her. Sex wasn't everything, but signs of love and affection were paramount to any relationship. It could not be considered balanced if only one partner enjoyed the offerings. Both had to be satisfied with what they were receiving. Tricia loved to give. She loved her role as Elias' wife. If she had her life to live all over again, her ministry to God and others would be the same; the only things she would change was the lack of affection she received.

"No-one important Elias" she replied. Tricia casually closed the flap to the phone case and slid it into her bag. She wasn't in the mood to talk to Elias. She hadn't even been in the mood to talk to Roger. He was trying too hard lately. Tricia enjoyed his company and his friendship, but she knew what his intentions were. He had made it clear that her happiness was utmost to none and he would stop at nothing to see her happy; even if that meant getting Elias out of the picture. Tricia wasn't ready yet to give up on her marriage. She had been down this road several times before. Every time she decided she would walk away and find someone else that better suited her, she would seize up. "Just for sex Tricia?" she would ask herself. "You are willing to walk away from your partner just because of sex?!" Once those thoughts climbed into her head she would chicken out. She could only imagine what the headlines would read in the local newspapers if word ever got out. Elias would be crushed and embarrassed. How could she do such a thing to him? That would have been the last straw. No man deserved the number of disappointments he had endured in life.

Elias continued to concentrate on the road. His wife's mood had not changed and he was getting worried. He wanted Tricia to enjoy this trip. It was the first one they had gone on together that would include vacation since their honeymoon. They pulled into the airport and parked their vehicle in the "Long Stay" area. This is where it would remain for the duration of their trip. Quietly, the two proceeded to the check-in counter and then continued to the travelers' lounge to wait for their flight to be called. There, Tricia indulged in a few glasses of red wine. Elias sat in the row of seats opposite her and just stared. He didn't know what to say or what to do. It was as if she was a ticking time-bomb waiting to go off. After about an hour of watching her, Elias got up and decided to walk around the airport. Their plane would soon be landing and then they could board and be on their way. While Elias took a stroll, Tricia took her mobile back out of her bag. She had felt the vibrations going off ever so often after she had placed it there. Taking out her charger, she plugged them in and checked her messages while she waited for her flight to be called. The plane had landed some fifteen minutes now and was being prepared for their flight. Looking through her received messages, Tricia realized Roger had blazed up her inbox. She sighed wearily. With knotted eyebrows Tricia replied to him with one stern message. "Roger, if you do not stop bothering me you will NOT see me on this trip! You can be sure of that! I am not in the mood right now to be harassed. Just give me some space to breathe PLEASE!!!" Tricia stared at the handset awaiting his reply. She saw a single "k" pop up on her screen and she began to relax a little. She opted to turn off the phone at this point as there was no reason to leave it on during the flight. Looking up, she saw Elias watching her from afar. He was leaning on the windowpane of the Duty-free Caribbean store. Smiling weakly, Tricia waved him over. She had to try to pull her marriage together. It was her duty. She couldn't falter at this stage. There was too much at risk and Elias, not Roger, was the man she loved. They would have to work it out one way or another. By the grace of God things will work out for them.

CHAPTER 20

The flight to Canada had been lovely. Elias had purchased some roses for her on his little stroll and this warmed Tricia's heart. Watching him look longingly at her gave her a new life. She tried to cheer up to enjoy the rest of the flight; and that she did. They ate a fine fare and drank a bit too much wine in their first class section. They had everyone in stitches; even the airhostesses. It was a party going on at the front of the plane. By the time they got off the flight, they had been on a first name basis with the entire section and the crew members. Tricia could not remember the last time she had so much fun with her husband. When they disembarked, they gave a solemn goodbye and everyone made their way to their various destinations. Exiting the airport, Tricia paused to take in the scenery and take a good stretch. Vancouver was pretty far from the Caribbean so it had been a long flight. Elias quickly hailed a cab and soon they were on their way. He escorted his wife to the hotel first and they both checked in even though he wouldn't be spending the first week there. Once he was comfortable she had settled in, he kissed her passionately and made his way to the community centre where all the priests and bishops would be gathering. It was going to be a hard week; full of services and ministry, but Elias was excited to be a part of it.

Tricia glanced around her lovely suite. Elias had really gone all out for this one. He had ordered several bouquets of flowers to be there on her arrival. The room smelt like a rose garden. Tricia loved flowers; this had gotten him big points. She moved from bouquet to bouquet now inhaling the wonderful scents. Passing her hand casually over a bloom, Tricia paused to take in the intricate detail of the rose. Funny how life is like a rose. You must go through the toughest of circumstances to bring out the beauty from within. She made her way to her private balcony. Opening the large glass doors, the Vancouver sun poured through the doorway and onto the carpet. It was almost lunchtime and Tricia was hungry. Lazily, she strolled over to the side table where several hotel documents lay neatly piled. As she was shuffling through for the room service menu, the phone rang and caused her heart to skip a beat. She was not expecting a call so she figured it must be Elias calling back to check on her.

"Hello."

"I see you have arrived safely." The voice on the other end was not that of her husband; it was Roger. Tricia had enjoyed her morning so much that she forgot to contact him.

"I am sorry Roger, I should have called." Roger had been annoyed when Tricia had pushed him away earlier but he needed to play his cards right if he wanted to win the heart of this Calvary beauty.

"No problem, I was just checking in to make sure all was well." He had just one week to make Tricia leave her husband. He could take care of her here in Canada; she needn't worry about having to face people when she returned home. They could start a family together. He had planned to introduce her to Timothy. The boy was already excited at the thought of meeting her. Roger had mentioned her after he returned home and told the boy he hoped to one day marry the woman. Timothy had been apprehensive at first. This was until Roger mentioned to him that Tricia would be more than happy to be his step mom. He had feared that Tricia would take Roger away from him; but Roger would have none of it. He knew oh too well how it felt to be deserted by the one man you looked up to. He was not about to do that to Timothy. "If she wants me it will be the both of us buddy," he had reassured the youngster. He was planning to get Tricia to fall in love with the idea of them being a family; that is, until they got children of their own.

"Are you up for visitors this afternoon?"

"Visitors? As in plural?"

"Yes, Timothy wants to meet you." Tricia paused. She had previously mentioned to Roger that she would be delighted to meet the young man, however, things were picking up for her and Elias again and she was beginning to get irritated with Roger's advances.

"Don't feel pressured if you don't want to Tricia. I would just tell him you're too tired or something." Roger could hear the hesitation in her voice. He didn't want to seem as if he was pushing her too hard. He was walking on eggshells around her. He could feel her pulling away from him and he couldn't afford for that to happen.

"No, that is quite fine Roger. I would love to meet Timothy!" At least the boy would be there with them so Roger couldn't risk anything. It was also safe for her if Elias ever found out. She had built a long distance relationship with the boy at Roger's request. She was actually beginning to enjoy the boy's company online. Timothy would have been crushed if she came to Canada and he didn't get to meet her. "You guys want to do dinner tonight?" Roger tried hard to hide his excitement.

"Sure my dear, we would love to!"

"Then it's a date. See you at eight Roger."

The line went dead on the other end. Roger disconnected his phone and ran to tell Timothy that they were going for a long afternoon drive to Vancouver. It would only take them a couple hours to reach there from where they currently were. Roger had rented an apartment for the week close by. He didn't want to travel too far to see Tricia, and he had planned to see her very often once she was in Canada.

Timothy put on his best outfit. He was excited to meet Tricia. Roger had been right about her; she truly was a beauty. They had spent many hours on skype calls together and had grown pretty close over the weeks. She was like the mother he never had so Timothy had gotten pretty hooked quite quickly.

"Whoa there fella," Roger joked. "Looks like you got a heavy date tonight!" Roger eyed Timothy from head to toe. He had planned they would have a manly vacation together and it had been going great so far. At his age Roger knew he would soon become interested in girls so he wanted to spend as much quality time with him before some young lady whisked him away. They had come up the week before and had spent the time doing several rugged activities. Now it was relaxation time before heading back to the rigors of work and school. The scent of the cologne he wore permeated the entire apartment.

"You need to look nice for a nice lady Roger. You taught me that," Timothy beamed proudly. Roger had gone all out to be a father figure to him and he never wanted to disappoint the man.

"Well, if I didn't know any better I would think you were going to meet the love of your life." Timothy blushed.

"I just want to look good for aunty Tricia." Roger knew the boy was looking to secure her friendship. He watched from a distance as the two of them created a bond that even he wasn't able to break. They would link up at a certain time each day and chat for at least an hour. At times Roger found himself becoming jealous at all the attention Timothy was getting from Tricia.

"You look great son." Timothy beamed.

"You look pretty good yourself Uncle Roger. Just a bit more swag and you would be as fly as me!" Roger playfully knocked the boy alongside his head at the sly remark.

"Well, all set?" timothy nodded.

"All set Uncle Roger." With that, the two set out to meet up with the beautiful Tricia Dessington.

CHAPTER 21

"Holy Shit!" Roger glanced up from his mobile and was about to chastise the young boy for the foul language when he noticed the reason for his exclamation. Tricia was making her way through the rows of tables and chairs in the upscale restaurant. Roger had chosen the fourth of the five restaurants that the Sandals hotel boasted of. It had just the right ambiance for a romantic dinner and just the right menu; seafood. Granted, with a third person tagging along it wouldn't be as romantic as Roger would have liked, but there would be other nights. Tricia was wearing a gorgeous outfit which had a sea of greens flowing into each other. The dress gave the effect of that of moving waves across the ocean. The colour, Tricia's favourite, complimented her complexion nicely. The strapless dress hugged Tricia all over and ended at a respectful length just above her knees. She wore a diamond butterfly set which glistened under the dim lighting in the restaurant. There was a matching diamond bangle on one hand and an exquisite Michael Kors watch on the other. Her hair was set in dropped curls which fell past her shoulders and tapered into the middle of her back. Roger watched her as she came towards them in a comfortable stride in some lovely high heeled pumps. God that woman was a sight to behold! Before he could say anything, Timothy was on his feet. Tricia smiled as she thought the youngster to be quite cute. Timothy pulled out a chair for Tricia to sit.

"Since when did you know how to be a gentleman?" Roger was shocked but pleased. He was sure Timothy would make a young lady very happy one day. He was growing into quite a fine young man.

"Good night gentlemen." Tricia showed a brilliant smile. Roger joined Timothy in a standing position as they waited for Tricia to accept the seat. Once she was settled, the two men resumed sitting.

"You are so gorgeous!" Roger's head swung over to where the gushing boy was sitting. He couldn't help but laugh as Timothy all but swallowed Tricia with his eyes.

"I have never seen a woman as beautiful as you aunty Tricia." Tricia blushed. She was accustomed to men looking at her, but never so young.

"Keep it up young man!" Timothy smiled. He looked up to Aunty Tricia even though she had been in his life only a short while. He hoped the two would get together and they could be a family one day.

The night went smoothly. Timothy stole the night with his jovial nature. He and Tricia laughed the night away, much at the expense of his Uncle Roger. Roger didn't mind; actually he quite enjoyed it. Watching the two of them interact brought him much joy. Tricia was a natural with kids. He imagined she would be quite the mother someday. Timothy had asked her why she didn't have any children yet. She didn't know what to say to the youngster. She assured him that if God had it in his plans for her, a child would be born. The next question wasn't expected by either of the adults.

"So how is your married life?" Roger was the first to react.

"Timothy! That is very rude." Timothy began to sink in his chair. He was hoping Tricia was having a horrible marriage and would come and be a mother to him. He knew it was a selfish thought but he couldn't help it.

"I'm sorry Aunty Tricia." Tricia regained her composure and smiled gently. The question had stunned her somewhat as she stared at Timothy speechlessly.

"That is ok Timmy." She didn't bother to answer the question. They sat and finished dessert and walked Tricia to her room. After a short goodnight, Roger thanked Tricia for a wonderful evening. She reached down and gave Timothy a bear-hug and gently placed her hand on Roger's arm. Planting a soft kiss on his cheek, she bid them both good night and closed the door to her suite.

On the drive back to their apartment, Roger was quiet. He had been in deep thought the entire ride and Timothy noticed.

"You're in love with her aren't you Uncle Roger." Roger chuckled.
What do you know about being in love chap?"

"Well, the way you look at her tells me a lot! Your eyes grow misty every time you mention her name and your voice changes." Roger began to deny it.

"You must have had too much sugar in your smoothie my boy. Aunty Tricia is married." Even when he said it he knew he didn't sound too convincing.

"That doesn't mean you're not in love with her. Don't worry, I love her for you too." The boy gave Roger's shoulder a knock with his fist.

"Funny how life can be so complicated huh? If she wasn't married, I'm sure you two would be together by now." Roger was sure of it too. No-one knew Tricia like he did.

"Enough of this sappy chat Timothy. Your job right now is to make sure I don't fall asleep on the drive back home!"

Timothy laughed. "Yes Uncle Roger." With that the two of them continued in silence. Their minds on the same thing; how do they hook the likes of Tricia Dessington.

Chapter 22

The rest of the week Tricia joined the boys on different tours and excursions. They travelled all over the country, even getting lost a couple of times. All in all they had fun. Tricia almost forgot that her husband would be arriving at the hotel the next night. Things had been pretty hectic for him with that crusade. Tricia attended a couple of the items on their list of events, but the majority didn't interest her. She hadn't seen her husband since they arrived in Canada. He had skyped her a couple times but she was usually out. By the time she got back home he was offline.

It was the Thursday night when Tricia had just settled into bed after a warm shower to do some research on her laptop. It was her way of unwinding. She was looking for a good book to purchase as she was out of new material. She had been with Timothy and Roger earlier that day at the water park and decided to order in dinner that night. At least she would have been available if her husband called. She usually left the machine opened just in case a message came through and she was available. Soon there was a knock on the door.

"That was quick" Tricia mumbled. Expecting it was a waiter from the restaurant with her dinner, Tricia wrapped the robe around her and quickly went to answer it. She was more than a little stunned by the visitor.

"Roger! How are you? What brings you by at this hour?" It was still early in the night, but Tricia wasn't accustomed to having visitors at that time.

"Is it too late for a visit?" Roger was eager to spend some alone time with Tricia. He had enjoyed the quality time they had spent together but was getting weary that they always had a third piece to the puzzle.

"No, not at all. Please come in. I was about to have some dinner. I thought you were the waiter."

"I didn't mean to disturb you but I was getting a bit antsy. We haven't spent any alone time together Tricia. Tricia softly closed the door behind Roger. She knew this would pop up at some point even though she had prayed to make it back to Calvary without being alone with him. She just didn't trust herself around the man.

"Look Roger, these past few weeks have been hard on me and I know we have gotten closer as a result. But I want to try to make my marriage work." Roger's head lowered involuntarily. "What happened between us was wrong and I don't want to lead you on."

"Wrong? How could it have been wrong when you enjoyed it so much Tricia?" Tricia turned her back to Roger now. She knew he was right but she couldn't make him think she would leave her husband for him.

"I don't want to confuse things Roger." Elias and I have been married for a few years now and we have established a life together."

"From the looks of it, it's not much of a life! You crave attention Tricia, I can feel it. That man doesn't have a clue how to cater to you emotionally; I do." Roger stepped behind her now. The scent of her coconut pineapple body wash still lingered in the air of the room from her bath earlier. "Let me be that man for you Tricia. Let me give you the experiences you have been waiting for your entire life."

Tricia's eyes closed as she felt Roger's breath in her hair. He placed his hands on her shoulders and began to massage her gently. Tricia shrugged him off. "Roger, I don't think this is a good idea…" Roger stepped back and gave her space.

"You don't want to make love to me Tricia? Is that it?" That wasn't it at all and Roger knew that very well. Even now there was undeniable electricity in the room. Tricia had always wanted to see what Roger would be like in bed. But she couldn't.

"No Roger, I can't make love to you." A smile spread across Roger's lips now.

"That is not what I asked you Tee Tee. I asked you if you don't want to…" Tricia's head hung low. She knew she had been caught. Roger could feel her desire pulling him in. Without a word he resumed his position behind her. He reached around her shoulders and cupped each breast with his hands. A gasp escaped her lips. Massaging gently, Roger leaned into Tricia's ears. "Tell me that you don't want me Tricia…" Tricia leaned back onto Roger's chest as her nipples began to perk beneath the terry robe. Pressing a bit harder now, Roger asked again. "I'm waiting Tricia. Tell me… or I will be fucking the shit out of you tonight." The words shook Tricia's very core. Her hands flew up now to cover Roger's own as he squeezed and plucked the rounded buds. With one swift movement he untied the robe from her waist. The halves dropped loosely exposing a tight tummy. Roger's hands shifted upwards to release her shoulders of the cloth and the robe fell to the floor. Now fully exposed to his eyes, Roger began to devour her. He sank his teeth deep into her neck and began to suck; his tongue lashing back and forth on her skin. While one had continued to assault a breast, the other reached down and grabbed her vagina as her ass rested on his firm penis. Tricia was overcome with sexual desire. It had been so long since she had sex and she knew Roger would deliver. What could possibly go wrong? The man lived in Canada after all. It would be their secret. He kept one before; this would just be another. The sex that followed belonged in the animal kingdom. They were so into each other that no-one heard the subtle knock of room service. The waiter could hear the commotion behind the door so he simply put the tray on the ground and pushed the bill beneath the crease. Roger was out to all. He finally had Tricia in his grips and he wasn't about to let her go. Ripping at his clothes, Tricia hastily tried to undress him. Standing naked face to face, Roger lifted Tricia with ease. Her legs spontaneously wrapped themselves around his waist. With searching eyes Roger looked for her consent. Without a word, Tricia dug her fingers into his head and kissed him passionately. It was all Roger needed to know. Resting her back against the far wall, Roger thrust deep inside Tricia. The force was so much Tricia yelped but Roger didn't stop. With her head bobbing back and forth with every thrust Tricia pleaded with Roger to give her more; and Roger delivered. Her nails dug deep in his back for support and Tricia wined her ass and willed him to go deeper.

"More Roger, more!" Roger Duncan was indeed in heaven. It was the moment he had waited thirty seven years for. Nothing could have stopped him at that point. Moving her from the wall to the bed, Roger worked Tricia over in every which way he knew how. When Tricia stopped to suck his dick Roger thought he would go mad. Tricia took him in and damn near swallowed his manhood. Grabbing a fistful of her hair, Roger moaned and grunted with each flick of her tongue. Where the hell did this woman get so much skill?! He was sure the Rev didn't get down and dirty like this. Even the language Tricia was using was filthy. "Let me suck you baby" she had pleaded. And when she wanted the dick she would come out right and let him know. "Fuck me Roger, fuck me harder!" When he first heard her he paused; not sure if he was sexing the right woman. But it lit a fire within him. He made her plead and beg for it; he loved to hear her voice screaming his name.

"You are behaving like a dirty slut Tricia… that shit is turning me on!"

"I am baby. I am your dirty slut. Come fuck me like one." Roger's dick leapt in anticipation. In a firm back-shot Roger smacked her ass going and coming. He had to hold on to her waist as the force with which she rammed back on him nearly threw him off the bed. God this woman was wild and sexy! How could Elias not turn this over every single night! If she were his woman Tricia would be walking as if she straddled barrels all day long! A natural "O" would form between her knees because he would be always between them. Roger sank his teeth into every inch of her body. He licked and sucked her all over; even her well-manicured toes. He just couldn't get enough of her.

After being all spent, the two collapsed on Tricia's bed. It was everything they had both imagined and more. Neither of them had noticed the blinking red light that flashed from Tricia's laptop.

Chapter 23

"Ring ring... ring ring..." The hotel phone jumped the two lovers from their slumber. They had worked each other over again that night so there was nothing left for them to do but sleep. The loving had been epic. Tricia had experienced orgasm after orgasm with Roger and he too was well spent.

"Ring ring... ring ring..." Tricia shot up to a sitting position now as the phone rang through the dead of the night. Roger rolled over and began to snore afresh. Rubbing her eyes to focus, Tricia noticed it was 2:47 AM. Who on earth could be calling her at that hour. Moving sluggishly now towards the phone Tricia's tummy rumbled. "Damn, I didn't eat my dinner" she remembered. Reaching now for the handset, she answered with as much vigour as she could muster at that hour.

"What the hell is so important at this hour of the morning?" It wasn't exactly the best of greetings but really, who could blame her. A muffled voice came through; one which woke Tricia right up.

"How could you do this to me Tricia... how could you do this to us?!"

"Elias?!" Tricia's eyes opened wide at the sound of her husband's voice on the other end of the line. Focusing hard now on her caller, Tricia asked him to speak clearer so she could understand what he was saying to her.

"You... you... how could you do that Tricia? How could you make love to him that way?!" Tricia was stunned. How could Elias possibly have known? Roger hadn't even left her hotel room as yet!

"What are you talking about Elias?" Something told Tricia she wasn't going to be as lucky as the last time. Elias sounded pretty hurt; as if he had been drinking as well. "Where are you?"

"Haaaaa where am I? Take a wild guess Tricia" came the drunken chuckle. "Guess where I am babe." Tricia roused Roger now feeling somewhat petrified. She had never heard her husband like this before.

"Elias you are scaring me."

"Why? Because I can see you and you can't see me? That shouldn't scare you Tricia. What should scare you is this here gun I have in my hand. Now that should scare you!" Tricia pounded now on Roger's back and he woke with a start.

"Yes, wake the scoundrel up! Let him join the party!" Elias laughed as Roger rolled over again.

"Roger GET UP!"

"What… what is it babe…" Roger sat up with a start.

"Roger, Elias is on the phone!" Roger rubbed his eyes, quite annoyed that Tricia woke him up for that!

"Why the hell would you let him know I am here" Roger whispered.

"Put me on speaker Tricia. NOW!" Tricia immediately did as she was told. Tears flowed down her face as confusion encompassed her.

"Don't play you are crying now woman! You weren't crying when he had you pinned to the wall! Ahahahahahahaahah." The look on Roger's face was priceless. He pulled the sheet further up under his chin; feeling very much exposed now.

"Where the hell are you Elias" Roger demanded, looking all around the room.

"Where I am is none of your concern mate. Where I am going though will be on your conscience for the rest of your life! I hope you can handle that my dear fellow!"

"He has a gun Roger" Tricia whispered.

"What are you talking about Elias? What are these strange comments you are making?" Tricia heard the cock of the gun.

"Well! As for you my dear Tricia… I hope you are prepared to explain to the masses why the death of the Bishop of Calvary is your fault! I clearly wasn't good enough for you Tricia, and from what I saw last night, I can understand why." Neither Tricia nor Roger could comprehend how exactly Elias had been able to witness the act of infidelity; but that was far from the point now. Elias was talking about killing himself and they both were scared senseless.

"Look man, you don't have to kill yourself! Some things were just meant to be. I guess this was one of those things…" Roger was making a futile attempt to bring sense to the madness. He never intended for things to get this far, he just wanted Tricia to have a good life. Roger explained as much to Elias before Tricia whacked him on the shoulder. His words weren't exactly helping the situation at hand. A wail came through the speaker now as Elias became overwhelmed with grief. The words were muffled but still audible enough to have a chilling impact on their audience.

"Don't tell me about making Tricia happy! When I asked her to marry me she was the happiest woman in Calvary! It is her love for sex… filthy dirty sex that has brought us here today. What else do I have to live for huh? Give me one good reason why I should not pull this trigger!"

"Look Elias, we can work this out honey." Tricia's voice was trembling. She couldn't imagine what her life would be like if Elias killed himself. That would be a controversy for the ages.

"Work this out? Work what out Tricia?! I have tried for the past few months to work this out!" This isn't the first time you have cheated on me! And I said nothing!" Roger turned to Tricia in shock. He knew something more had to be going on but to hear that Tricia, precious Tricia, had a history of infidelity was simply too much for him to swallow at once. Tricia hung her head in shame. How on earth did Elias know about this? Her eyes shifted from left to right trying to jog her memory as to when he might have indicated he knew; she was clueless.

"Tricia… what is Elias talking about?" A hearty chuckle came through the speaker now.

"Oh! You didn't know that you were just one of her many lovers did ya?" Roger clenched his teeth at the thought. Tricia didn't strike him as the kind of woman to run around so Elias must have been mistaken! Ignoring the man on the phone, Roger asked again.

"Tricia?" Tricia's body began to shake as the tears flooded down her face. Her whole world was becoming unravelled and she didn't know how to make it stop.

"I… I don't know…"

"You don't know?" Elias boomed! "What is it exactly that you don't know Tricia? You don't know how I found out about Cincinnati? Or is it that you don't know how I found out about Kansas? Oh! Maybe you don't know how I could possibly know about Nigeria! Now Nigeria was definitely one for the books Roger! That one made your performance look like a dance! But the best, I mean the absolute best was Marcus… wasn't it Tricia?" Tricia clutched at her chest. This was definitely too much for her to handle. Her husband spilt all of her recent exploits, and even though it was only Roger in the room, she felt exposed. She opened her mouth to say something but no words came out.

"Ahhhh speechless I see. I tried to ignore it you see. I tried to fool myself that it was someone else committing these disgusting acts; that it couldn't be my wife. I didn't want it to come to this, but even after I sent you that letter you didn't stop! You just wouldn't stop Tricia!" Tricia could hear Elias choking on his words as he tried to keep himself composed. Tricia's eyes bulged. It was her husband who had penned that letter to her; but how did he keep it all together? It must have been so hard for him.

Forcing herself to respond, Tricia sputtered, "But how Elias, how did you know?"

Elias chuckled again. "You know Tricia, I may be a man of God, but I know things. You literally stopped making love to me Tricia. After you tried to get me to do some of these nasty things to you, you became unresponsive. It was as if making love to me sickened you! I saw that change Tricia and I investigated. There is no way that a woman tries to entice you one night and then gives up sex for months after she didn't get what she wanted!" Tricia didn't realize it was so obvious. She just would lie there and let Elias do his thing before she rolled over and carried on. His love making did nothing for her.

"Do you know how it feels to see your woman literally withdraw from you? Do you have any idea how I felt that night after you tried to sexually attack me? I knew within myself that I could not be living up to your standard, but I tried! In my own way I tried! I tried to make love to you more often, but you blanked me; completely! Tricia felt awful. Elias had felt rejected all this time but said nothing. There were still so many unanswered questions but the pieces of the puzzle were beginning to come together for her. Roger sat in silence. He was in awe at the tragedy that was unfolding before him and he didn't know what to do or how to feel about it. This was no longer about him making love to a married woman; this was about the married woman, who was so sexually frustrated that she stepped out; several times!

"I have a confession to make." Tricia looked over to the phone and waited expectantly. "Actually, I have two confessions to make!" Tricia knew she wasn't going to like this one bit. Elias's words became increasingly slurred as he took another swig from the rum bottle. He dropped the gun on the table with a thud which made Tricia jump.

"I, my love, have turned into a prime investigator." Tricia's eyebrows began to knit in the middle as she tried to understand what Elias was going on about. "Yes my dear, though I may not be able to sex you as you would like, I was able to make good use of myself." Roger was thoroughly uncomfortable. He had never seen such a pathetic situation as this one, and though he didn't care much for Elias Dessington, no man's inefficiencies should be exposed to another in such a manner. He actually felt sorry for him right now.

"You see, being a Bishop gives you access to people in all walks of life see, especially criminals. It is our duty to counsel these persons, and more often than not, when they leave prison, they feel grateful that you helped them turn their lives around." Tricia didn't like where this story was heading one bit. She sat quietly and let Elias ramble on.

"So one day, God sent me an angel. Yes, I call him an angel. Because that day, I was at my wits end trying to figure out how to make you love me again. But I had prayed to God and asked him to show me the extent of this situation, as at the time I was still clueless. I didn't know at that point what wickedness you were getting yourself up to! So along came my angel, and instead of me counselling him, he counselled me. He told me that I have always been good to him and now was his turn to return the favour. Though apprehensive at first, the need to know what was going on to my once loving wife was overwhelming, so I accepted." Elias paused to take another swig. Both his listeners sat still, waiting for the rest of the story to surface. "So, so in all of 5 minutes my boy hooked me up!" Elias chuckled again. "Within 5 minutes, I was able to see every single thing you did on that blessed laptop!" All eyes now swung in unison to Tricia's opened laptop. Her mouth dropped open involuntarily.

"You had me hacked?!" Tricia asked in disbelief.

"Not only hacked my dear. I can also see your every move once that machine is positioned properly! So I not only had access to your emails, but I could see you from anywhere in the world! How cool is that Tricia?" Tricia was horrified. Her own husband placed a tail on her. He so much didn't trust her that he thought it necessary to do this; and rightfully so!

"How could you do that Elias?"

"How could you hire those men to fuck you Tricia!" Tricia jumped. Elias never swore a day in his life. Either the alcohol was getting the better of him, or he was pretty angry right now.

Roger's eyes turned to Tricia once again. "Hire? I was here trying to be with you for years and you PAID other men to fuck you?!" Roger was slightly disgusted. His entire image of Tricia was crashing around him now.

"Not the innocent little princess you thought she was eh Roger?"

Tricia started to get upset. She needed to defend herself. It wasn't like she was some kind of slut! She wouldn't allow herself to be dragged through the mud without a fight!

"Listen to me! I tried with you Elias! You know I did! I tried everything in my power to entice you! No woman should have to work so hard to make her husband want her!" That was the truth if ever Roger heard it. Tricia wasn't exactly that easy to ignore either so he was at a lost as to how the man was able to restrain himself.

"I was never a sex animal Tricia, you know this! The things that Roger and Marcus did to you, I cannot bring myself to do!" Roger found himself wondering about this Marcus guy. What exactly did he do to Tricia? He knew now that she had a healthy appetite, but Elias was making it sound pretty rough.

"I don't need you to be an animal Elias; I need you to have an open mind! We are always in the same position! I never get to have fun! You cringe at role play, you cringe at oral, and you cringe at everything that I tried to do with you. What exactly did you expect me to do?! Roger lowered his head. While this was pretty amusing to him, he didn't think it was appropriate to be snickering.

"So you opted to get these services from other men?!"

"Again I ask you what was I to do Elias. It has been years we have been married and I am yet to be sexually satisfied by my own husband!" Tricia raised her voice now. He had to see how his actions contributed to this mess. It couldn't fall squarely on her shoulders. Of course, she was wrong, but in marriage there must be compromise, and so far she had experienced none as it relates to this area.

"So this is my fault Tricia? Are you trying to say I forced you to have sex with other men?!"

"Well I didn't bring them home #1, and #2 I didn't form any relationships with them. I respected you during this entire fiasco Elias. I respected you and your position! I went to great lengths not to be caught; not because I would be embarrassed, but how would it look if it got out that the Bishop can't service his own wife! After everything that you had been through in Grenada, do you think you could have handled that Elias? I refused to do anything on island. I refused to be with anyone that you knew. Roger was a mistake because it has been so long that I actually sought pleasure, but this was not intentional! This you probably know already since you have been tracking my every move!" Elias knew she was right about certain things. For one, last night was the first night Roger had been in her room. Secondly, she hadn't made any appointments in a couple months for some reason. But all the rest was swimming above his head. Did this mean that she should be excused?

"I tried Elias, you know that I tried!" Tricia continued. "I approached you, my husband, on several occasions. I tried to bring spice into our love life; wanted to try new things, but you rejected me! Each and every time, you rejected me! How do you think I felt Elias? But instead of looking for another relationship, I looked to fix my problem and still be a wife to you! I never allowed my activities to affect my duty to you as your wife. Yes, I know I was wrong, but what option did you leave me with Elias? You know that I love you! Everything that I do in life I do for you! Though wrong, I did that to keep me sane. I am sorry that I hurt you Elias, I really am. That was certainly not my intent." Elias sat quietly and listened to his wife. Roger rolled out of the bed and began to get dressed. This was out of his league. Tricia still clearly loved her husband and this issue was not one that should be fixed with him in the room. Secretly, he wanted to escape before Elias could do anything stupid.

"Look guys, I am going to leave so you can thrash this out. This has nothing to do with me. Tricia…" Roger didn't even know what to say to the woman. He looked at her through different eyes now; unsure of what to make of this entire thing. Turning towards the computer screen, Roger acknowledged Elias. Elias stared back at the man as if he could see into his eyes. "Elias, for what it's worth, I am sorry you are going through this. For my 2 cents, that woman loves you, and you should do all in your power to make this work." Quickly throwing his shirt over his shoulders, Roger made clean his escape.

CHAPTER 24

The room was quiet now except for the quietened sob coming through the phone line. Roger had left Tricia and Elias to work their situation out by themselves. Tricia didn't know what to say to her husband. She had tried so hard to avoid this, but now everything collapsed. She felt awful, but she had to address her needs as well. She knew she couldn't be the only woman in the world in her shoes right now. Not that it excused her behaviour; she just needed to be understood and maybe, get help. She had to make her husband understand that she still loved him dearly. She wanted to make love to him, not these other men. She didn't even want to be with Roger, he needed to understand that. On the other hand, Tricia was sure that what he saw last night would remain with him until death. Her main concern now was to prevent that death from happening by the work of his own hands! Where on earth had he gotten a gun from anyway! Her husband didn't own one of his own; at least not that she knew about. He must have contacted one of his people here in Canada. This entire situation opened a serious can of worms. How could she trust her husband again? And how could he trust her? They both were in a grim position of distrust. The devil had been hard at work in their marriage, and must now be enjoying the fruits of his labour. Suicide is the ultimate sin. It is as if you are flying in the face of the Lord who gave you that life. Life is a blessing, and you should never let the pressures of life bring you to the point where you think you are worthless. You are never worthless to God!

"Elias…" Tricia reached out to her husband. She couldn't let him kill himself. They needed to overcome this. In a way, Tricia was happy it was all out in the open. The burden of keeping such a secret was tiresome.

Elias snapped back to focus on his computer screen. In a matter of minutes his wife had looked weary. Still a beautiful woman, Tricia's eyes were puffy from the constant crying. She had looked so fragile sitting alone in the bed. He wanted to believe her; he wanted to believe that everything would be ok. But how could he go on? Roger had gotten his hands in his business yet again! Tricia knew that if Elias got out of there alive today, the amount of work required to get him back on a stable path would be monumental; but she had to convince him that he was her world.

"Elias, I am so so sorry. I know my words may not be worth much at this time, but I need you to understand that I had no intention of hurting you." Elias could see the sincerity on Tricia's face. "I swear, if you kill yourself I would not be able to carry on. This has nothing to do with me Elias. I chose you as a life partner because I wanted to be with you. I wanted you to be the father of my children; to be the one that I wake up beside every morning and go to bed with every night. I wanted us to experience love and life together. It is you I said yes to Elias, no other man. You cannot imagine how sorry I am about this entire thing. I was wrong; totally wrong and I don't know what to say to make you see how much you mean to me. I don't know what to say that will erase the things that you saw, the distrust and the lies. I would do whatever it takes to get us back onto the road of recovery, but I can't live without you Elias."

Elias rubbed the back of his head as he listened to his wife confess her sin and her love for him. How the hell was he going to make this work? He knew he was not man enough to take his own life. He had just wanted to feel powerful in this awful situation; to feel like a man again. It had been brutal to watch his arch enemy ravish his wife; and she loved it. That is what sent him over the edge. He had sat and cried throughout the entire thing. And as much as he willed himself to look away, he couldn't get past the immense pleasure on his wife's face. After pulling himself together, he packed his laptop in his bag and had roamed the streets that night. He walked into a more unsavoury area in Vancouver and enquired about purchasing a gun. With all the money left in his wallet, he made the purchase and got himself a room in a nearby motel. It was all a farce and he knew it. A man that took a cat to the vet that he accidentally brushed with his vehicle was now going to try to take his own life? He was only fooling himself and he knew it. But his message got across and that was what was important. The look on his wife's face told it all. He was glad she was unable to see his though as he was a royal mess.

"What now?" The question startled Tricia. She thought she was losing the battle with him. Treading cautiously, she made a few suggestions to help them move on from here.

"First of all, I think we need to cancel this vacation and have a long talk; just the two of us. We need to understand the magnitude of everything that has happened so far. Secondly, we need to think about what this all means for our future… if you still want to be my husband I mean…" Elias hadn't thought about giving up the marriage. He really didn't know what he had planned to do afterwards.

"Thirdly, if you do decide to forgive me and want to make this work, we need to find a counsellor that we can trust." Elias nodded as if she could see him. This was going to be one hell of a journey and he knew it would take lots of work. He probably should have sought counselling before. Both of them had their own demons to fight with and would need help to make sense of it all. As he often told the men that came his way, never be ashamed to say that you need help. It is when we keep things bottled up inside that they eat away at our very being. It is healthy for men especially to reach out when they feel burdened.

"Ok." Elias didn't have much else to say. He knew she was right. They could get over this if they worked hard at it. He didn't know if he could open up more sexually, but he had to be willing to try. She was willing to give it all up just to be with him and make things work. Didn't he usually tell the women that came for counselling because of infidelity that God would help them through once they committed to his love and mercy? He wasn't exempt from life's issues because he was a Bishop. Elias sat lost in his own thoughts. At times, when life throws us difficulties, we forget the Almighty. We forget that we can trust in his name. Instead of snooping on his wife, Elias should have gone to God. When he had realized that his wife had deviated, instead of writing her a letter and hoping that she stopped, he should have nipped it in the bud and worked with her to come to a solution before it got further out of hand. Christians have to fight that good fight daily or the rigours of life would overcome them and stifle their ability to worship and praise their Father.

Chapter 25

"I speak to you in the name of the Father, and of the son, and of the Holy Ghost. Amen. Please be seated." The congregation sat as Elias took his position in the pulpit of the King James Anglican Church. It had been three months since he last was in that pulpit; in any pulpit for that matter. After the situation played out in Canada, Elias had gone back to the hotel with his wife. The two of them never saw sunlight again until it was time to check out. They spent the entire time talking and reconnecting with each other. Tricia had been pretty shaken up by the entire thing. It only goes to show, that as much as we do wrong in our lives, we are still fragile beings; God's creations. Elias admitted that he would need help in overcoming this hurdle, so they decided on who would be the one to counsel them on their return. As soon as they touched on Grenada's soil, Elias wrote a letter indicating he would be on medical leave for a few months. This was endorsed by a doctor who examined him and found his blood pressure to be sky high. During those three months, the couple focused on rebuilding their marriage. It was a struggle and only the beginning of a very long journey.

"I won't be speaking to you today from this pulpit," Elias began. "I will come down on your level. And by the end of this sermon, I suspect each of you will have a better understanding of why I did what I did." Elias was about to speak from the heart. He left his iPad which he usually read his sermon notes from and he activated the clipped portable microphone which was on his collar. The congregation all looked at him in puzzlement. Motioning to an altar server to come towards him, Elias proceeded to disrobe in front of the congregation. There was a hushed conversation breaking out across the church now as people began to wonder where the Bishop was taking his message today. The only person who looked straight ahead was Tricia Dessington. He removed his Mitre and handed it to the server. Next, he removed his cloak. Finally, he removed his robe and stood before the congregation in a lone shirt and pants as an ordinary man.

"Now, my friends in Christ, what you see here standing before you this morning is a man... a mere human being. Forget that I am a Bishop for just a few moments, and take a walk with me." Elias proceeded to walk down the aisle of the church and looked directly in the eyes of everyone that he passed.

"My message to you today my friends is simple. I am a man; nothing more, nothing less. What does this mean? It means I too am privy to the strains and struggles of this life. It means that I too feel the pain that each of you feel when something has gone terribly wrong in your lives." The congregation now began to hold onto every word that Bishop Dessington was preaching.

"You know, I once forgot that I was just a man. I forgot that I wasn't above the struggles of this life. And my friends, I forgot to go to God when things got rough. And do you know what happened my friends in Christ? When I forgot that Jesus Christ was my Lord and Saviour, do you know what happened to me?" The congregation now all shook their heads in unison.

"The devil came in and almost took me away from my God!" there was a hushed gasp. To hear the Bishop speaking about the devil coming after him was practically non-existent.

"Yes my people, the devil came after me and not in a little way, he came in for the kill!" the passion in the Bishop's voice placed them all on edge.

"I get up here and I preach to you about the sins in this world. But I forget to take stock myself! Can you imagine? I behaved as if I was too good for the devil to come after me! But oh no my friends. The devil was waiting. He was sitting in the dark and he was waiting for the right time to poison me!" Every neck in the church was turned towards the lone man in the aisle now; even the children were quietly listening.

"When the devil got his hands on me, he planted doubt. And that doubt grew and grew and festered like a cancer! That doubt grew until I almost lost my mind; and by extension my life! Yes my friends, what I am about to share with you, is a spiritual fall which almost took my life!" Elias paused to sip some water from the glass provided by the altar server.

"You see, I forgot I had a friend in Jesus. I forgot that in times of trouble, I could lean on him. 1 Peter chapter 5 verse 7 reminds us that we should cast our cares on the Lord because he cares for us! I forgot to do that my friends in Christ. Instead, I chose to try to fix things on my own. Have you ever tried to fix something that you weren't an expert at my friends?" Several people nodded. "And how did that turn out? It was a disaster right?" Even more nodded in agreement. "Well when I tried to fix this problem in my life, all hell broke loose! Instead of casting my cares on the Lord, I tried to read those instructions myself and I failed miserably. Not only did I fail my friends in Christ, but I was almost damaged to the point of no return! You see, when Satan saw that I wasn't going to ask Jesus for help, he stepped right in to help me. I didn't ask him either mind you, but God reminds us that we should always come to him in times of trouble; and I didn't. So I left the door wide open for Satan to get into my life!" Many heads in the church were bobbing up and down. The sermon was speaking to many congregants and Elias was reaching out to them in a different way. "Now tell me, if your car breaks down, don't you go to the mechanic? And if you want bread to eat, don't you go to a baker? What about if you need financial advice? Don't you go to a banker? Or in illness, don't we go to see a doctor?" Heads nodded again with each question and response. "Why then is it so hard for us to go to God when our souls are going astray? Isn't he the one that made us and not we ourselves? So shouldn't we reach out to our maker and say "Lord fix me!"? Instead, we figure we can fix these things ourselves but end up making a royal mess of our lives!"

"Well let me tell you my friends, when Satan gets a hold of your life, he doesn't let go! You have to wrestle with him to get back your life out of his grasp! But don't fear, the Lord reminds us in Philippians chapter 4 verse 13 that "I can do all things through Christ who strengthens me." Repeat that with me." The congregation repeated the biblical verse as requested by the Bishop. "Yes! I can do all things through Christ who strengthens me! How many of you believe that? How many of you believe that God can give you the strength to overcome anything in your life?" Several hands flew into the air.

"That one little verse speaks volumes my friends in Christ. It tells us that the day that we are feeling down, God will be there to pick us up. It tells us the days when we don't think we can take another failure, God will be right there to lead the way. That little verse dear friends reminds us, that when we stumble along life's path, God will be there to get us back on our feet again! When you are about to say "I can't" God is saying to you "Come my child!" When you are saying "This won't work" God is saying "Let me help you!" You see my brothers and sisters; God is there with us each and every step of the way. We just need to accept his help!"

There was a resounding "Amen" from the crowd.

"I want each and every one of you to do something with me today." The Bishop motioned to the ushers who had large rolls of bounty paper towels in their hands.

"I want each of you to take a few sheets of paper towel. Don't be shy. Take a sheet to represent a problem that you are going through right this very minute. If you think you need a whole roll take it! We have more!" Amused, the congregation quickly accepted the paper towel sheets so as to participate in the rest of the sermon.

"Everyone have their sheets?" The ushers nodded and returned to their places, taking their own sheets of paper as well.

"Good, now that we have our sheets we are going to do a heap of wiping today. We are going to wipe away the negativity from our lips brothers and sisters. For the man who thinks he can't walk the straight and narrow road in his marriage I want you to wipe your lips and throw that paper on the ground and say YES I CAN! For the woman who thinks she can't break that shopping habit that she has I want you to wipe those lips and say YES I CAN! For the child who doesn't believe they can pass those final exams even if they study just a little bit I want you to wipe your lips and say YES I CAN! Everything that you have going on in your lives this very moment that you think is keeping you back, just take that blessed paper and wipe your lips and say YES I CAN! I CAN give up that drug addiction! I CAN forgive my friend! I CAN leave that woman's husband alone! I CAN stop stealing from my workplace! I CAN be nice to the neighbours. I CAN be an honest individual." Soon the church was abuzz with everyone in their space wiping and throwing their doubts away.

"The Lord told me that I CAN so YES I CAN! Don't let Satan come and tell you no! Don't let Satan make you feel as if it's the end of the world! I want you all to shout GET THEE BEHIND ME SATAN! Come on! He needs to hear you!" Joining the Bishop, the congregation all shouted "GET THEE BEHIND ME SATAN!"

Elias continued in a renewed spirit now. "He WANTS you to fail! He WANTS you to give up! He WANTS you to keep sinning brothers and sisters in Christ! Don't give him a strong hold in your life! Cry out to Jesus today! He will save you! Say LORD, HELP ME! I'm SINKING! Go on! Reach out to the Lord your God and ask him to help you through whatever it is you are battling with today!" Hands reached towards the ceiling in praise and glory. "If Satan had his way I would be a dead man today praise God! But I thank the Lord that I remembered Him, AMEN! I thank the Lord that I remembered he is the way, and the truth and the LIFE! I thank the Lord that I remembered to come to him before it was too late! Before Satan snatched my soul and added me to his kingdom!" By this time people were jumping and skipping in the church and praising God. Some had fallen to their knees in prayer. The spirit took over the church and not a dry eye could be seen as the congregation prayed to God for deliverance.

Pausing a while for the church to settle down a bit, Elias continued. "My friends in Christ, I am a sinner. I come to you today as a mere mortal. I stand before you as a man who has made some horrendous mistakes in this lifetime. But as a man, one of God's children I am not above asking for forgiveness. When they nailed Jesus to the cross he said "forgive them Father, for they know not what they do!" Jesus knew we were sinners, he knew we would need forgiveness. We should not be afraid to ask for that forgiveness. We should not be ashamed to say "Father, forgive me for my sins" and mean it! Mean it from the very core of your souls my brothers and sisters. Mean it as if your life depended on it! You just stood with me and confessed to the Lord that you CAN be a better person if you tried. From this day onward, let your journey be about making that a reality. Let every action you make this day forth, take you one step closer to God's kingdom and away from the grasps of Satan." Elias closed off his sermon and began to make his way to the front of the church. "In the name of God the Father, God the Son and God the Holy Ghost. Amen"

As Elias concluded his sermon Tricia rose from the kneeling position she had maintained throughout the duration. While she hadn't moved a muscle, she had prayed more zealously than she had in ages. She asked God to forgive her for her sins. She went humbly before Him as her husband had; without title. She bowed her head and went to the Lord as Tricia; the woman who faltered in her marriage. The woman who did wrong and now wanted help to get on the straight path again. As the tears flowed down Tricia's face, she maintained her composure. She was proud of Elias. They both had undergone some intensive counselling from two specialists; a marriage counsellor and a sex therapist. The marriage counsellor was able to help them work through the lack of communication in their marriage. Though they spoke every day, they never discussed the issues and things built up until they would go their separate ways. The Sex therapist was able to help Elias open up about sex in his marriage. Instead of seeing these acts as dirty, he was able to better understand his wife's needs and cravings. They were given several activities to do together, including watching educational sex videos. Elias was able to see and appreciate how certain sexual scenarios pleasured his wife. Though they still had quite a ways to go, Elias had opened up much more and Tricia was enjoying her new husband. They both took small steps towards catering to each other's needs and as a result had begun to create a stronger bond in the marriage.

Elias passed his wife on his way back up to his seat in the altar. He paused just briefly to glance at her. She was still as beautiful as the first day he met her. If one thing was for certain, Elias had planned to do all in his power to keep his marriage going on the right path. There was no turning back now with God on his side!

About the Author

Jasmine Christine is an up-and-coming author who decided to take all her moving ideas and put them onto paper. Her style addresses real-life, everyday issues while enticing the reader with juicy erotic clips to whet their appetites. Life is a journey, and one that most persons barely endure instead of enjoy. Jasmine grew a great fascination of how man and woman fought against the odds to join as one in the name of love. At the age of thirty years old, Jasmine has decided to step out of her box and enjoy this journey. Jasmine's overimaginative mind propelled her to try her hand at her own fiction love story. As a proud Barbadian, Jasmine has only dared to exist within the confines of her structured upbringing. Her second novel "The Bishop's Wife" is one that, in her mind, aggressively touches on things lived but unspoken. With an ever-active imagination, this novel was born. Look out for more erotic novels from Jasmine as she takes flight into the world of words.